Life in a Slower Lane

by

Joan G. Creager

Cover Photo by Barb Seibel.
Author Photo by The Camera Shop.

"Life in a Slower Lane," by Joan G. Creager. ISBN 1-58939-374-0.

Published 2003 by Virtualbookworm.com Publishing Inc., P.O. Box 9949, College Station, TX 77845, US.

Manufactured in the United States of America

For John

CONTENTS

Homing In On Home

Finding the right home in the right town has created monumental dilemmas for many retirees, and my husband, John, and I were among them. We moved six times before we homed in on a honey of a house in the congenial community where we now live. From 1987 to 1996, we floundered about in a tumultuous odyssey of living arrangements and locations, always believing every move was our last. Our search began when John retired, I became semi-retired, and our children had found homes of their own. The brick colonial in Arlington, Virginia had served us well for twenty-six years, but it was just a house and we had no qualms about selling it. We were ready for life in a slower lane. We wanted to stay fairly close to our adult children, especially our daughter, the single parent of our two granddaughters. We wanted to be part of their lives without interfering.

"Should we look at apartments?" I asked as we sat over breakfast reading the *Washington Post*.

"No, let's not," said John. "We'd be at the mercy of a landlord and our rent would pay for someone else's property."

"Scratch the apartment. How about buying a lot and building a house?"

"Where would we find a lot?"

"I don't know. Let's see what's available," I said as I rummaged through the classified ads. "Listen to this. Five acre lots, easy forty minute commute on I-66."

"Who wants to mow five acres? Or drive I-66 to visit the kids?"

"No, I guess we don't."

After that discussion, we looked at condominiums, and settled on a ground level, 2-bedroom, 1½-bath unit in Fairfax, Virginia. We moved in the spring of 1987 and quickly learned to like living a few miles farther from Washington's rush hour gridlock. The condo had a summertime swimming pool and grounds maintained by the staff. It was near our daughter and not too far from any of our three sons.

We were content at the condo for nearly five years while our granddaughters grew into junior and senior high school. Both came after school on Fridays and spent the night. We played board games and card games, and I made costumes for school programs. Traffic worsened with the turn of each calendar page, and we found ourselves in a snowless, urban heat island.

That plight set us looking for a small hideaway in a snowy place. We soon found another condominium near the summit of Blue Knob Mountain in Pennsylvania, about a three-hour drive from Fairfax. It would be snowy in winter, cool in summer, and usable year round. We bought it. We knew we would enjoy a heated pool, walks on wooded trails, and a fireplace like the one I had missed since we sold our house. Once we started exploring the area, we fell in love with the gentle mountains, restful valleys, and the less hurried pace of life.

Returning to Fairfax one evening, we encountered a massive traffic jam.

"John, why are we doing this?" I asked as we inched through a cloud of greenhouse gases.

"Why are we doing what?"

"Putting up with all this traffic, that's what."

"To be near our granddaughters. I thought that was why."

"Well, it was when they were small. But they rarely visit us now."

"They have their own activities. That's the way things should be."

"I know. It's time we had our activities, too. In a more congenial place. Why don't we move to Pennsylvania?"

"You mean live in our hideaway?" John asked in a surprised tone. "It's too small and too isolated. Seven miles to a store and twenty to a doctor."

"No, not there. Maybe a town with a college like Purdue where we met."

"Hmm. Let's think about it."

We pored over maps and located college towns in Pennsylvania. We reminisced about Purdue–walking together on campus, visiting the creamery, meeting for coffee, and spending evenings in the Union lounge with John playing the piano. We remembered our first dances together–when Benny Goodman or Guy Lombardo played "big band" music in the Union Ballroom. I tingled with joy at the prospect of living where I'd be reminded of those days.

We settled on State College, the home of Penn State University. State College is located only sixty miles from our hideaway and no more than 200 miles from any of our offspring. Although no town could restore all the accouterments of our blossoming love, this one offered cultural events, libraries, light traffic (except on football weekends), and a creamery. This creamery has the best ice cream we've had since we patronized the Purdue Creamery in our courting days. It rotates seasonal flavors like blueberry cheesecake and pumpkin pie, but it maintains a year round supply of standbys like butter pecan and John's favorite, mint chocolate chip.

Now that we had a town, we needed a home. Another condo? All the condos were occupied by students with beer kegs and stereos. We wanted to be close to college life, but not that close. A small house on a small lot? In the dead of winter and in the middle of an academic year, few houses, large or small, were on the market. Maybe a factory-built modular home? My spunky mother bought one when, at 81, she found herself with no family nearby. She set her home on a lot near my brother and enjoyed the rest of her days there.

When our real estate agent told us (erroneously, we discovered later) that State College frowned on modular homes, I thought about designing a house. We bought a mountain-view lot on the edge of town on New Year's Day, 1992, and put the Virginia condo up for sale. I became a self-appointed architect, and we visited our mountain getaway and State College often to check on the house. One Sunday we visited the local Unitarian

Fellowship, where John met a colleague he hadn't seen in thirty years. That made our new town start to feel like home. When the Virginia condo sold, we moved temporarily to our getaway until the house was finished in June. By fall we knew more people in State College than in any other place we had ever lived.

Winter brought my long anticipated snow–a record-breaking 110 inches. I adored every flake! Along with the snow came the first disappointment in the house. Our two-sided fireplace looked like the one we had enjoyed one winter in a rental house, but it didn't act like it. Instead of a cheery fire, we sometimes got a houseful of smoke. Our second disappointment came in the spring when that old urge for a vegetable garden grabbed me and held me in its clutches. Maybe I have a dirt-digging gene that's activated by the availability of dirt. At least, I thought I had dirt, but I found only rock thinly veneered with not very fertile soil.

While we worked to solve the house's problems, we kept meeting nice people who lived in a continuing care community.

"Come on over and have dinner with us," said one of our new friends in the community.

"That would be nice," John said.

"How about next Saturday night?"

"We'll look forward to that," I said.

"Come to our cottage for a drink before dinner and we'll give you a tour of our facilities after dinner."

Part of that tour included a view of the auditorium with its concert grand piano–a real Steinway. When John learned that residents could play that piano, he was ready to move right in. After several discussions of the pros and cons of the community over two years, I reluctantly agreed to move in *if* we traveled for a year first.

We sold the house in May 1995, stored our furniture, and became vagabonds. I loved "vagabonding" in our charmingly rustic, 15-year-old camper, a tan-and-white 19-foot Dolphin built on a Toyota pick-up truck chassis. It had a bed over the cab, a sofa bed, two barrel chairs, and a pedestal table. Across the back were a phone-booth-sized bathroom and the essentials of a kitchen. All this convenience in 90 square feet, and 17 miles per gallon of gas to boot.

We headed west and revisited Rocky Mountain National Park while snow still blanketed the mountain peaks and adorned the evergreens. We explored Canyonlands, Redwoods, and Roosevelt Parks, and touched base at some old favorites. On our anniversary, we dined at the Bryce Canyon Lodge, where we clinked our glasses "to another good year" for the forty-third time.

All too soon the time we allotted to the west was gone, and we returned to our mountain condo in August. We stretched out on a real bed and got rid of our travel kinks. We collected our mail and paid our bills. John got his annual physical exam. Wham! His physician diagnosed atrial fibrillation and hospitalized him to regulate his medication. We feared our vagabonding was over. A week later John was free to travel, but we committed ourselves to the retirement community before we set out for our last four months of freedom.

We enjoyed autumn glory from New England through Cape Breton to Newfoundland and met our goal of visiting every Canadian province. We spent Thanksgiving with family in Virginia and headed south to join a tour of Antarctica, our seventh continent. We flew with the group from Miami to Argentina. There we boarded a former Russian research vessel and rolled and pitched across the Drake Passage to Antarctica's awesome, snow-covered peaks.

As I looked out our stateroom window, almost mesmerized by the grandeur of those mountains, I said, "John, I almost can't believe we've really made it to this place."

"It is a dream come true."

"Yes, indeed. Just look how the midnight sun paints those peaks in glowing pastels."

Every day we donned our boots, boarded a rubber Zodiac, and made one or two "wet-landings" by throwing our legs over the side of the raft and wading ashore. When the resident penguins spotted us, they interrupted their squabbles over nests to waddle toward the shore and form what looked like a receiving line. The chinstrap penguins, named for a thin row of black feathers that gave the appearance of a broad grin, entertained us with antics like climbing small snow-covered mounds and sliding down on their tail feathers. All too soon, we had to say goodbye to Antarctica and head home.

Our vagabonding was over, but for me, it had been a peak experience of my life. I thrived on anticipating and then experiencing each destination. Having almost no housekeeping chores was a relief, but having no fixed address was downright exhilarating.

Then came that fateful day. We paid our fees to the retirement community and chose the least inconvenient of the available cottages. No mountain vista here, just a fine view of the community fire lane. We moved our furniture on a blustery first day of February, and I immediately began the struggle to put my heart into the place. While John played the Steinway in the auditorium, I worked in our cottage, covering institutional-white walls with pictures or wall paper. Every day at breakfast I looked out on fifteen identical front doors, all with frumpy old people just like me behind them. No toddlers, no school kids, no teen-agers. No young adults hurrying to and from work. Just old folks puttering about. Administrators less competent than I managed my life and served up mail, meals, and "meds" with all the grace of well-oiled automatons. Living in that geriatric ghetto seemed like an unnatural act and I soon reached the end of my tether.

"John, I love you," I sobbed, "but I can't live here. I'll get an apartment and visit often."

He stared at me. "I'm sorry you're not happy. But we belong together."

"I know we do and I'm sorry, too."

By morning, John had decided that what he really needed was a good piano. We stopped at the office to give notice on our way to look at houses–and pianos.

I learned a lot from that experience. Each time new residents move into a cottage, the property owners receive an entrance fee equal to the market value of the property. This allows them to collect the value of each cottage over and over. When I toured the nursing home component of the community, I realized I'd rather be dead than live there. So I developed a plan: Specify in a "living will" what life-prolonging medical services I did and didn't want under various circumstances. Give a younger, strong-minded relative or trusted friend medical power of attorney to make decisions if I can't. Move into a house or condominium. Faithfully invest the savings in living expenses compared to community fees. Under this plan, I, or my representative, would retain control of my money and my choices.

We implemented that plan and moved in June 1996 to what I think really is our retirement home. It's an easy-to-care-for house on a small lot in a modest State College neighborhood. We have neighbors of all ages and front doors of all descriptions. John soon had his new piano and he began to play it every day. Last season my garden produced twelve gallons of strawberries and enough vegetables to finish filling a large freezer.

The house has everything we need on one floor, a finished downstairs for parties and guests, an attached garage, lots of mature trees, and a relatively small lawn. We installed new windows, remodeled the kitchen, and enlarged the living room to accommodate the piano. That piano fulfilled one of John's dreams at a time when we need to fulfill lifetime dreams before we run out of lifetime. I feel positively pampered in this honey of a house. Of course, I'll go vagabonding again if I get a chance, but I'll come home to this house. And my heart will still be in it.

On Getting a Medicare Card

One bleak November day, I poured a cup of coffee and sat down to read my mail. Ah, ha, a letter from the government. I opened that one first.

"Egad," I said to John. "I just got my Medicare card."

"Oh," he said without much feeling. "It happens to everybody if they live long enough." He's was already accustomed to having his card.

My body quivered as that card dragged me willy-nilly into senior citizenship, as it pushed me into life in a slower lane. No matter how much we seniors make light of mounting years, calling ourselves old geezers or geezerettes, aging is real. It's both a burden and an opportunity.

Looking at aging as a burden, I lament the fact that my body is becoming less dependable. My hair is white, my skin is wrinkled, and I move at a slower pace. My hands have age spots and lumpy knuckles. My tummy sags, my joints creak, and I have trouble getting to the bathroom in time. But that doesn't mean I must give up and drag my rocking chair into one of today's warehouses for the elderly.

I've been reading up on aging. Part of it is built into our genes. A second part is in our environment–harmful agents such as toxins that poison our brains and internal organs, ultraviolet rays that cause skin cancer, and a host of other factors. The rest is the lifestyle we create through choices we make–what we eat and whether we exercise. We can't do much to change our genes, but we can work to clean up our environment and make healthy choices about our lifestyles. Beyond that, it doesn't pay to let the burdens of aging overshadow its opportunities.

Aging brings retirement, and retirement offers a golden opportunity—the chance of a lifetime to do the things we've always wanted to do. But it's not an everlasting opportunity. Actuarial tables show that the longer we live, the longer we're likely to live. Even so, every day is precious. That Medicare card reminds me about precious days. It goads me to decide what things I most want to do and to get busy doing them.

Foremost, John and I will continue to honor the promises we made nearly fifty years ago to love, honor, and cherish each other as long as we both shall live. We will make a point of doing things together knowing that someday that may not be possible. We're not crass or sentimental, neither morbid nor maudlin, just realistic about senior life. Each of us hopes to leave good memories to sustain whoever survives alone. We've made a faltering effort to videotape the best photographs we've taken during our years together. If we can improve our technique we will have tapes to share with each other now and to freshen the memories of whichever of us survives alone.

We don't intend to live on memories alone. After a time for grieving and healing, whoever survives will pursue his or her own interests. Each of us has a consuming interest, something we like to do for its own reward. My husband's special interest is music. He plays the piano, attends concerts, and listens to recordings. He sang in a chorus until after his seventy-ninth birthday. Mine is writing. When I'm immersed in writing, I lose track of time, forget where I am, and become completely engrossed in what I'm doing. Making a piece say just what I want it to say gives me great satisfaction. I jealously guard my writing time lest ubiquitous interruptions fritter away the hours and leave me wondering as I crawl into bed where the day went.

My computer is an essential tool for doing several things that are important to me. I use it in my writing, of course, but I also use it to keep in touch with family and friends, search the Internet for information, and make travel arrangements. To get on good terms with my computer, I took adult classes at the local high school and the public library. Some class members were scared of computers at first, but we all finished knowing a computer is just a machine that does what we tell it even if we tell it something absurd. Computers can be exasperating and befuddling, but they are also infinitely patient and never critical. Anyone can learn to use a computer and most libraries provide free access to computers for their patrons.

In addition to John's music and my writing, we share a passion for travel. In fact, travel is the one thing that can draw us away from music and writing for days and weeks at a time. We spend many happy hours reminiscing about trips we have made and planning new ones.

"Where should we go next, John?"

"Let's rest up from the last trip before we start planning the next trip."

"Okay, but I can think about. In fact, I have been thinking about how to travel. I've just about had it with air travel, and I think we would enjoy our travels more if we take our car and plan easy days."

"I agree with that," John said emphatically. "I'm always game for a trip to New England if we stay out of cities."

"So am I. And I like Canada, too."

"Yes, but enough for now."

We who live on the North American continent are blessed with travel riches. We can take advantage of the world's greatest assortment of national, regional, and local parks, lakes, seashores, rivers, and monuments, each with scenic, environmental, or historical attractions. When we looked close to home, we discovered that our adopted home state of Pennsylvania had 116 state parks. We decided to get acquainted with the state by visiting every park. After many day trips, a few overnight trips, and eight years, we achieved our goal.

When we don't want to travel independently, we sometimes travel with Elderhostel, a non-profit organization that provides programs for seniors at various locations in the United States, Canada, and many other countries. Beyond making sure participants are well-fed and comfortably housed, these tours offer sightseeing, challenging lectures, opportunities to make new friends, and the joy of leaving the shopping to others.

By juggling our travel dates to avoid summer crowds, I can be at home to plant and tend a garden. Maybe it's my farm girl upbringing, but I still like to watch seeds sprout and grow and I rejoice in the earthy odor of moist soil as it rolls before my tiller. Enjoying the fruits of my labors compensates for the aching joints that come with gardening.

Writing, traveling, and gardening are important benefits of retirement, but there are more. We retirees can speak out on issues without worrying about what the boss thinks or how the neighbors will treat our children if they disagree with us. I speak out mainly by offering workshops on population. I'm convinced that if we don't stabilize human population, a burgeoning population will make it impossible to solve environmental problems. I also write letters to the local paper and commentaries for the local PBS radio. These and other volunteer activities make me part of a larger ongoing effort that will continue after I'm gone. My work will blend with the work of others and what I help to accomplish will live on after me. That gives meaning to my life now and will make letting go easier when I'm dying. Maybe it will also help give meaning to my life for family members and friends who survive me.

We seniors have spent much of our lives giving to our children and to the people we work with. Now it's time for us to practice receiving for we are likely to depend on others someday. I hope to do this graciously and appreciatively so my helpers can experience the joy of giving. For now, I've got lots of living, loving, and giving to do. So I'll tuck away that Medicare card and be thankful for the gentle prod it gave me to get on with my life.

On Exercise

Now that I no longer hustle through my days, I've been forced to resort to exercise as an essential pastime. Unless we seniors make a special point of it, we don't get as much exercise as we got when we were working and raising families. Worse yet, our metabolism tends to slow down more than necessary and we accumulate fat. Physicians tell us to exercise to control our weight and keep all our joints working. I suppose that's good advice and I try to follow it. But that doesn't mean I enjoy it. I hate exercise. Not quite as much as I hate cooking, but I really do hate to squander time on exercise. For me, nothing I find interesting is good exercise, and what's good exercise isn't interesting. Exercise will never be my favorite pastime.

Now that I have fewer commitments, finding time to exercise is not the problem. Finding motivation is. Somehow, getting exercise through productive work is less loathsome than getting exercise for its own sake. Doing housework, tending a garden, mowing the lawn, or running the snowblower all are good productive weight-bearing activities. Pushing a pen or keyboarding my writing provides exercise for my mind and fingers, but that's not physical exercise, the *real* exercise I need to stay healthy. The only solution to the exercise problem is to get up and move, even when I have nothing productive to do.

Different activities appeal to different people. I hate the awkward expression "different strokes for different folks" but it does express what I'm trying to say. For me, the least evil form of exercise is swimming. Other marginally tolerable kinds of exercise include riding a stationary bike, walking, and working out with an exercise video.

Long ago when our children were young, my husband and I took them swimming every day in the summer time, and we swam, too. For over twenty years, we've had access to a year-round pool and we've gone swimming three times a week, except when we were traveling or when the dressing rooms were so cold they made our bones ache. I used to swim half a mile each time I went to the pool. Now I swim half an hour, which as I lose speed amounts to gradually decreasing the distance I swim. I'm determined to continue this routine as long as I can.

Swimming really is good exercise. It uses many different muscles without putting great strain on any. Although it's not weight-bearing, it stretches every muscle and seems to let tension flow out of my body and wash away into the depths of the pool. I get the kinks out of my muscles and the creaks out of my joints. I must admit that I feel a moment of ecstasy when I step into really warm water on a very cold day.

Unfortunately, stretching and relaxing aren't enough. I must keep moving, up and down the pool. It gets deadly dull with the same scenery for every lap—pool tiles in the foreground and exercise equipment in the background. Now and then, just to break the monotony, I do a lap or two of backstroke and count the big white sheets of fiberglass that form the suspended ceiling. Using their 2 by 4 foot dimensions, I put my mind to work calculating the length, width, and area of the pool. Also doing backstroke, I try to predict when I'm coming to the end of the pool in time to turn just inches before I bump my head. Every few round trips I time myself. Twenty years ago I could to do a round-trip in forty-five seconds. Now it takes me fifty-five on a good day and a full minute on a not-so-good day.

By the time I've been swimming for half an hour, my body has adjusted to the buoyancy of the water and I feel heavy and ungainly as I hoist myself up five shallow steps to get out of the pool and eight steep ones to reach the ladies locker room. Once I'm showered, shampooed, and towel-dried, I force my still slightly damp body into ordinary street clothes. Another day, another swim. My virtuous, self-satisfied smirk must be disgusting to see.

Recently, when my husband's doctor told him to get more exercise, he added a stationary bike to our exercise arsenal. I've tried it. Simply pedaling round and round watching the needle on the timer slowly creep along would do for a definition of the ultimate in boredom. In fact, riding that bike goes right off the top of my boredom scale. It makes counting ceiling tiles at the pool seem exciting. The best remedies we've found for bike boredom is to play music or read a book. We moved an ancient stereo system and our long-playing record collection downstairs near the bike. *Eine kleine* Mozart or some folk music does a lot to raise my spirits above the boredom of pedaling. And if all else fails, I can pick up a travel book and pedal off to a far away place.

Walking is good exercise, probably the best weight-bearing exercise we seniors can do. My husband and I have several different walking routes we can take in our neighborhood or in nearby parks. I almost enjoy a short walk in spring when the first flowers of the season are coming into bloom or in the fall when the trees are in full-color. I also like a short, exhilarating walk in winter if there's an ice-free place to walk. In summer I get hot, sweaty, and bug bitten. My surgically mangled foot makes it impossible for me to honestly say I really enjoy any of these walks. When I have a chance to travel to new places and must walk to see the sights, I grit my teeth and trot right along. Only my passion for traveling and visiting new sights can overcome my lack of enthusiasm for walking.

A few years ago I bought an exercise video for seniors. Doing the same exercises over and over with the same people in the video is so boring that it's acceptable only on windy, icy days in the dead of winter when there is no yard work and walking in the neighborhood or driving to the pool is hazardous. Some good things about exercising with the tape are that it works all major muscle groups and it can be done regardless of the weather. What really "bugs" me is that when I watch the people on the tape, I feel like the people on the tape are watching me, too.

In spite of various ruses to disguise exercise, it's all fundamentally boring. But so is work like vacuuming, tilling soil, pulling weeds, and deadheading spent blossoms. All are humdrum, but exercising as I do chores at least accomplishes something worthwhile and it usually involves a variety of movements. I suppose I will finish out my days contending with the evils of exercise lest my joints freeze up and sentence me to a rocking chair, or worse yet, a wheel chair. But I can't help thinking it's a darned shame that exercised is so good for me.

Flappy Foot

My surgeon gave me a "flappy foot." It flaps about like a wet sock when I try to take a step or bend my ankle. I didn't ask for it. I didn't appreciate it. But I had to learn to live with it.

The events that led to flappy foot with its dysfunctional family of toes started when age-related osteoarthritis caused me to seek a second hip replacement. (The other hip had been replaced in a different city six years earlier.) I wish I had known about glucosamine-chondroitin sulfate, a concoction of ingredients found in normal cartilage and joint fluids, before I agreed to the second surgery. I would have tried it and I might have avoided the surgery and the nerve damage that caused my flappy foot.

I asked for the surgeon who was currently performing the most hip replacements. Instead, as I later learned, I got the one who had done the most over his long career. He had a reassuring manner, and I confidently scheduled surgery with him. The operation took place.

The next thing I knew, I was floating up into the misty, half reality that follows general anesthesia. I expected a semi-private room, but as I started to come around, I felt I had wandered into somebody else's family reunion. I got my eyes to focus on a teen-aged girl in a robe and slippers. It was no trouble to focus my ears on a loudmouthed woman I assumed was her mother. A sea of faces–probably brothers, sisters, aunts, and friends–swirled in my dizzy brain and sort of ran together with the din of multiple conversations. Whoever they were, they filled every bit of space short of sitting on my bed. I was so happy to hear the mother say,

"Aggie's going home tomorrow," that I quickly shot up to a higher level of consciousness. Suddenly, I realized I had a bigger problem than that roommate and her noisy family.

My foot was on fire! A sheet barely touching my foot fanned the flames almost to the flashpoint of a scream. Something had gone very wrong during surgery. Each time a nurse or aide came into my room, I called attention to my problem.

"My foot's on fire," I said. Nobody understood. I was a "hip" and they all knew that "hips" didn't have fiery feet.

"It'll be better tomorrow," they said, but they didn't really take my fiery foot seriously. Had I been able to rise above the fire in my foot, I would have expressed my rage at their insensitivity and patronizing attitudes.

After a long sleepless night, daylight came and with it my breakfast. Soon a cheery nurse popped into my room. "It's time to go for a walk," she said.

"Walk!" I exclaimed. "I can't walk on that foot. I can't even bear to touch that foot."

"Oh, yes, you can. Everybody walks the day after surgery. It's safe to walk on your new hip as soon as the glue is dry. Let's get going."

"But that *foot* isn't ready to walk on," I protested. "Something terrible has happened to the nerve to that foot. It feels like it's on fire."

"Well, let me see," she said as she patted my toes. I screamed. Now she was sure I was a hysterical hypochondriac. "You can tell your doctor later, but now we must walk."

I winced as she shoved a slipper on my throbbing foot. She set a walker next to my bed and I stood on my good foot. Flappy foot hung down like a limp rope from a limb on a hangman's tree.

"You've got foot drop," she said in an accusatory tone that seem to say I had maimed my own foot just to make her job more difficult. Later, a more sympathetic nurse taught me to hold tight to the walker and stand tip-toe on my good leg while I swung flappy foot forward. Finding somebody who cared lifted my spirit like nothing else had done.

Midmorning my surgeon appeared at the foot of my bed. When he turned back the sheet, I winced. “Don’t touch that foot,” I said.

“That’s what we call foot drop,” he said as he stared at the foot. “I’m sure I didn’t cut that nerve.” He explained that only four of the 8,000 hips he had replaced had foot drop and three of those recovered spontaneously. How MY foot would function remained to be seen.

Later that day a nurse brought a foot brace. “Doctor’s orders,” she said, as if that explained everything. Then she proceeded to stuff my fiery foot into the brace.

The next day the surgeon sent his assistant. “That’s not the right brace,” he said.

“Take it back. It only makes matters worse anyway.”

“We can’t. It has already been used. But I’ll have your doctor order a different one,” he said as he hared off.

The second brace was no more helpful than the first. Medicare would be billed about $500 each for two useless braces and I would still have a fiery, flappy foot.

Quite soon my surgeon discharged me and sent me by ambulance to a rehabilitation center near my home. I’m sure he was glad to be rid of me. Traveling by ambulance was like being shipped by *UPS* or *FedEx*, dependable but impersonal and not very comfortable.

The physical therapists at the rehab hospital were more attuned to needs like mine. They listened to me and carefully assessed the nerve damage. They prescribed exercises to help me cope with the paralysis. They also discovered that the operated leg was nearly an inch longer than the normal leg. No wonder I had trouble swinging that foot forward. Now when people asked me how tall I was, I could ask, “Standing on which leg?” That thought made me laugh for the first time in a week. The therapist had an inch-thick sole glued to shoe for my normal foot. That made walking a little easier, but a one-inch heel would have been a less clumsy way to solve the problem. They were doing the best they knew how.

So were the nurse’s aides, but they didn’t know much. They were programmed to perform mechanically, just like robots, and weighing patients was part of the Saturday program. My aide, Miss Day Robot, parked my wheel chair and waited for me to hop onto the scales.

"I can't get on the scales by myself," I said. "I need a walker to help me keep my balance while I swing this flappy foot onto the scale."

"Oh, I'll help you," she said in a reassuring voice.

I trusted her and tried to step up. Flappy foot dragged on the edge of the scale and I fell backward. She caught me, but not before my head was near the floor and my foot was set ablaze. Some time after midnight the pain subsided enough for me to sleep. Way too soon after that, Miss Night Robot found a castoff brace and woke me up putting it on my foot. A day or two later, Miss Muscle Robot slammed flappy foot into the leg rest on my wheel chair. I screamed. A bevy of robots converged on my room but Miss Muscle had disappeared. When the doctor in charge of the Robot Stable came to my room, I said, "I can't stand any more of the kind of help I'm getting. I'm going home."

Doc admitted that he couldn't hold me against my will. But he insisted on getting an x-ray of the foot to make sure that my foot had not sustained additional damage. He also had a cast made for a third brace. Had that foot really been the flaming torch it felt like, the technicians would have set the whole place on fire maneuvering my foot into various ungainly positions. Eventually, the Afternoon Robots helped my husband get me to the car and we headed home. He and some special friends helped me hobble into the house and to bed.

By morning the nerve had quieted enough to let me inch along solo on my walker. Except for trips to the dining table, bathroom, and bed, I spent most of the next month in a straight-backed, upholstered chair in our living room. Special friends brought tasty food and good cheer. The technician from the rehab hospital delivered the brace he had made from the cast. I used it for a few doctor's appointments, but it was set at such an acute angle that I had to bend my knee with each step. Now I had a third useless brace. That made me wonder how so many well-meaning people could have bungled into so many frightful errors.

After I'd been home about two weeks, my brother and sister-in-law came from Michigan. They cheered us up, helped around the house, took us out to dinner and for a ride in the country. They readied the yard for winter. And they didn't bungle anything.

By the time they left, the leg with the flappy foot had gotten hot, red, and swollen, just like when I had phlebitis after my first hip replacement. The local orthopedist, who couldn't find time to see me, sent me for a sonogram to check for a blood clot in the leg. None was found. The orthopedist did nothing more, so I went to my primary doctor.

She took one look at my leg and said, "Hot, red, and swollen. That leg's infected. I'll give you an antibiotic."

"Sounds good to me. It's great to have you actually look at the leg. I thank you."

"Just doing my job," she said. Her tone reflected the self-confidence of one who knows how to do a good job and does it. Soon the infection was cured.

The leg still tingled from knee to toes as if I had been sitting on it, and the only ankle-bending muscle in a human leg remained paralyzed. I saw a local neurologist several times. He did everything he could to wake up that dead nerve. In spite of his real compassion and valiant effort, nothing worked. Somehow over time, the too-long leg got shorter. I cut the thick sole off the shoe for my good foot and put a half-inch lift inside it.

When I heard of a highly recommended orthopedic shop, I got a fourth brace and a pair of oversized brogans. One brogan held the thick plastic brace. Its mate held the lift and enough stuffing to keep the shoe from falling off. For about a year, I wore the brace and brogans when I had to walk, but I walked as little as possible.

Finally, I retired the brace and brogans and took matters into my own hands. I bought high-topped hiking boots, laced them up, and tied them tight. Then for the flappy foot shoe, I ran an extra shoelace from the bottom eyelets cris-crossed to the top eyelets. With the foot flat on the floor and the ankle passively bent, I tied the second shoelace. That kept the ankle bent and stabilized the flapping foot. I could walk with a nearly normal heel-to-toe gait.

To adapt the idea to other shoes, I made a padded ankle strap with an eyelet at each end and tied the second string from the bottom eyelets of the shoe to the ankle strap. I found similar ways to wear a variety of shoes and walk more naturally than with any brace. With a short rest now and then, I can walk whenever I need to. That's what I call victory over flappy foot.

A Writer's High

I sustained a Writer's High for months after I attended my first writer's conference in Philadelphia. My spirit soared. I felt exhilarated by the many ideas rattling around in my head. A new spurt of motivation infused my body with energy–energy to write, that is.

I registered for the conference months ahead of time. My husband, John, agreed to go with me. I told him I would worry about him at home alone and he said he would worry about me driving that distance by myself. It was easy to decide to go together. Shortly before we were to leave, I got a touch of "cold feet." What business had I dragging John along to while away three days in a hotel lobby during which I would attend sessions? But my feet didn't get quite cold enough to make me to cancel out.

We hit the road near daybreak to arrive for a 9:30 session. We were right on schedule until we drove through downtown looking for a right turn onto 4th Street and suddenly found ourselves on the Ben Franklin Bridge irreversibly headed for Camden and an unplanned tour of a massive riverside construction site. I was furious with myself for missing the turn. John, bless him, said something consoling. Otherwise I might have yielded to my momentary overwhelming urge just to forget the whole thing and drive straight home.

Fortunately, there really was a policeman on the corner when we needed him. He gave us directions to the bridge. On the way back across the bridge we discovered our turn was ever so easy to find. It's a simple right turn from the bridge –*if* you're coming from Camden. Eventually we found the hotel, parked, and agreed on where to meet for lunch. I soon knew that coming to the conference was the right decision and worth all the hassle of getting there.

Among the sessions offered, I chose a series on magazine articles, another on memoirs, and a third on books. The first series featured a magazine editor with a down-to-earth way of getting her points across. "First you need a good idea," she said. "That's an idea you can turn into an article that will sell. You've probably passed ten good ideas already today. Pay attention. Eavesdrop on conversations. Carry a notebook. Use it."

"Second, you need to know where to publish your good idea. Study the market." That means making such a thorough analysis of the format and content of various magazines that you can detect nuances between very similar magazines, such as *Family Circle* and *Women's Day*. Ah, ha, I thought to myself. I can do that. It will be tedious, but I can do it. Already I was fired up to get started analyzing magazines and revising essays to fit particular magazines.

At the memoir series, the speaker talked mostly about good writing. "Use all your senses when you write," she said. "Help your reader see what you see, hear what you hear, and feel what you feel." She gave us ten minutes to practice using all our senses in a personal essay, starting with: "I was standing barefoot on the cold linoleum floor when . . ." I enjoyed the writing, but the real fun was hearing participants read their different stories. My mind was swimming with ideas for how I could liven up my essays.

Next the speaker offered a three-step writing technique: pre-writing, free writing, and shaping. I've been practicing at home. In pre-writing I collect facts, dialogue, and images about a topic. In free writing, I set a timer, say, for ten minutes, pick up a pen, and "let 'er rip." No editing, no stopping to think, no worrying about organization, just writing. In shaping, I underline powerful words and phrases and discard garbage. I repeat these three steps until I develop a piece and polish it as near to perfection as I can get.

Next came the book writing series. The speaker there had written several historical novels. He drew everyone into the discussion when he read from a list of 19th and 20th century inventions and challenged listeners to say when common objects were invented. Which do you think came first, the wristwatch or the fountain pen? Well, the pen came out in 1884, twenty-six years before the wristwatch in 1910. How about contact lenses and cellophane? Which came first? It surprised me to learn that the lenses appeared in 1887 and cellophane not until 1904. Our speaker made his point: know the times about which you write. He also fired up my enthusiasm for revising my historical novel, *Pigeon Roost*.

Everyone at the conference had an opportunity to meet with a literary agent. Mine listened intently to my carefully rehearsed presentation. But then she shook her head and said, "Your essay collection would be easier to market if it had a single theme. My heart fell as I recalled how hard I had worked to organize the essays into five sections. Then she asked if any of my essays had been published, and I had to answer, "no." I thought I was out of luck, but the agent offered to consider marketing a book of essays if they were focused on a single theme and four or five had been published in reputable magazines. Her recommendations confirmed exactly what I had learned from the rest of my experiences at the conference. That was a reassuring confirmation that I'm on the right track.

By the end of the conference, I had experienced a kind of gestalt of ideas from the various sessions. The pieces fit together. I floated out of the conference tingling all over. I was on a writer's high. I still get tingles up and down my spine and butterflies in my stomach just thinking about all the things I had learned and all the things I wanted to try.

Tertullian's Blessing

I first became concerned about the human population explosion when I was still in the fast lane–teaching biology at a community college in the 1970s. World population had just passed four billion when I read about Tertullian, a third century C.E. lawyer and theologian who claimed that population growth was a scourge on humanity. His wry words have been dubbed Tertullian's Blessing:

The strongest witness is the vast population of the earth to which we are a burden and she can scarcely provide for our needs; as our demands grow greater, our complaints against nature's inadequacy are heard by all. The scourges of pestilence, famine, wars, and earthquakes have come to be regarded as a blessing to overcrowded nations since they serve to prune away the luxuriant growth of the human race.

World population was probably less than one million when Tertullian wrote those words. It now exceeds six billion and it's still growing. The main problem with a growing population is that more people means more poverty, even in America where affluent people enjoy some of the highest living standards in the world and poor people live in squalid conditions in inner cities and isolated rural areas. Over the decades I've paid attention to population trends, poor women have experienced increasing difficulty in limiting the size of their families. Having more children than families can support always results in poverty. Conditions are heart-wrenching in poor countries such as Tanzania.

Let me take you on a vicarious trip to Tanzania, one of the world's poorest countries. Our plane lands in Nairobi and we arrive by tour bus at the Kenya-Tanzania border. While we're stopped for a border check, a crowd of young mothers gathers around our bus. They tap on the bus windows to get our attention and beg us to buy handmade necklaces and trinkets. There's Mahti in the red print dress. Her baby rides on her back and her pot-bellied toddler with pipestem legs clings to her skirt. Most of the people on our bus don't realize that Mahti's trinkets are her only source of income. Mutare, her man, hasn't been able to find work for many months. At least he helps with the daily chores of gleaning food, carrying water, and gathering dung patties for fuel. Some of the men in their village don't help anymore. They are either too discouraged, or worse yet, infected with AIDS and too ill to work.

Mahti, Mutare, and their children live on the edge of starvation. The baby gets enough protein from Mahti's milk, but the toddler's pot belly is a sign of severe protein deficiency and malnutrition. After her baby came Mahti tried to get contraceptives from a health care center, but now the center has none. Mahti doesn't completely understand why not, but the aide at the center tried to explain that some powerful men in America stopped family planning funds because they feared the money might be used to pay for abortions.

"What can I do?" Mahti asked.

"I don't know," said the aide.

Mahti walked away with a look of desperation. "If I get pregnant again, I'll need to go to that unsanitary village hut where other women have gotten abortions. That scares me because so many women who went there have died. I'll have to either risk that or go through another pregnancy and watch as the baby I already have become emaciated and pot-bellied, too."

Mahti is only one among hundreds of thousands of women who live in the poorest countries of Africa, where one in ten newborns dies in its first year. Conditions are only slightly less desperate in poverty-stricken parts of India, Pakistan, Afghanistan, East Timor, Laos, and Myanmar. Making reliable contraceptives available to the women who want them in all poor countries would be one of the cheapest, most effective means of raising the living standards of the world's poorest people.

The United States is hampered in its efforts to help poor women by its own lack of an effective population policy, one dedicated to protecting the dignity of families at home and throughout the world. Such a policy is needed because humans stand alone as the only species that has liberated itself from most natural means of regulating population. The numbers of other species are limited by predation, lack of prey, flood, drought, or another environmental disaster that humans can usually protect themselves from. Because the size of human populations no longer determined by natural means, we humans must take responsibility for controlling our own numbers. Thus we need a population policy that encourages humans to voluntarily keep their numbers within limits that will protect the environment and allow the survival of other species. We must remember that we're not the only species on earth and we're dependent on many of our planet's other species for food, shelter, and other necessities. Even species that are not part of our food chain are, nevertheless, part of the complex and beautiful web of life of which we are part.

The miserable lives of families like Mahti's demonstrate the consequences of bearing more children than a family can support. That is the plight of 45 percent of the world's population who subsist on less than $2 a day. In fact world population today is already more than twice the number our planet can support at the level of affluence of Americans. We Americans must recognize that our failure to help improve the lives of the poor increases the risk that people who have lost all hope will stage revolutions against the affluent. It seems to me that the attacks on the World Trade Center and the Pentagon were the first steps in that revolution.

What to do? First, we need to work with other affluent nations and give as generously as we can to help poor countries stabilize their own populations and improve their living standards. We already know that a combination of free, easily accessible contraceptives and family planning information helps give women more control over their lives. This combination is also the best known method for preventing abortions. Simply making birth control pills cheap and easily available without prescription worldwide would help the 120 million couples in developing countries who want contraceptives but cannot get them. As physician Malcolm Potts wrote in *Population Press*, "The world would be a healthier place if oral contraceptives were available at every corner store and cigarettes were limited to prescription use."

Second, we need to put the abortion issue in perspective. No other nation in the world is so "hung up" on the issue of abortion as is a minority of U. S. citizens. Our planet simply lacks sufficient resources for every human to bear as many children as they are capable of producing. It's time we asked ourselves how an abortion could be more wrong than giving birth to a baby and watching it starve? More wrong than a mother dying from an unsanitary abortion and leaving orphans behind? Or more wrong than a child dying of starvation, lack of medical care, a parasitic infection from drinking polluted drinking water, or being bitten by malaria-infected mosquitoes? The fact is that we live in a dangerous world, and abortion isn't the most horrendous of those dangers.

I've grown old arguing for human population stabilization. Sometimes I can't help getting angry with people who oppose family planning, and I need your help. You and I, and anyone else who cares about the world we leave for our young people must speak out in favor of family planning. We must find ways to get the attention of elected officials, religious leaders, and newspaper editors. To keep focused on this task, let us each memorize the face of a healthy, loved, and wanted child–our own child or grandchild, or any child. If we keep that little face in mind whenever we call, write, or speak out for family planning, perhaps we can turn the tide to bring human population in line with the resources available to sustain it. Tertullian identified the problem two millennia ago. It's time for us to work together to solve it.

Coffee, Tea, a Bit of Wine for Me

Part of adapting to a slower pace of living is learning to sip and savor beverages, be they coffee, tea, or a bit of wine. Both my husband and I were coffee lovers when we met half a century ago. During the many years that we lived a fast-paced life, we bolted down our coffee on the run. Now we're learning to sip and savor whatever we drink.

Brewed coffee is a special treat in these days of instant everything else. No other beverage can quite take the place of freshly brewed coffee. Instant coffee is tolerable if it's the only coffee available, but it's really a different beverage, or so it seems to me, and it comes in a distant second to real brewed coffee. Sipping a cup of freshly brewed coffee ranks high among life's most special pleasures. My pleasure starts when I smell that wake-up juice as it drips into the pot. It brings me to full attention in the morning, and the first sip assures me that it's going to be a great day. No matter how far short of the mark a day falls, brewed coffee gets it off to a great start.

Now I have a confession to make. Like many other seniors and some not-so-seniors, I must limit my coffee drinking mostly to the decaffeinated variety. At the time I drink coffee I can't tell whether it's decaffeinated or regular. Only later, after I have rolled and tossed half the night, do I realize that somehow I have imbibed some coffee with its caffeine intact. This is most likely when I have eaten in a restaurant where someone made a mistake about the coffee. After more than fifty years and drinking thousands of cups of high-test coffee, I guess I've already enjoyed a lifetime caffeine quota. I'm content to finish out my days with decaf.

The most comforting way to drink coffee is to hold the cup in both hands just under the nose so as to savor both its aroma and its warmth. Then set the cup down and stir in a smidgen of milk—not cloying fat-laden cream that overpowers the coffee–only a little milk to enhance the flavor and take the edge off some small bitterness. Finally, it's sipping time.

Now that I'm retired, I sip every cup of coffee slowly. Having time to sip coffee doesn't mean that I have nothing important to do and must find ways to kill time. In fact, sipping coffee is a way to do two important things at once—savor coffee and savor time.

The business of savoring time comes naturally with aging. Now we're trying to learn to savor tea as we savor time. In fact, my husband and I have been experimenting with tea. John sometimes drinks green tea. Green tea is supposed to be better for us because it contains a strong antioxidant that wards of cellular deaths that contribute to aging. Drink it, enjoy it if you can. I'll give you my share. I prefer black tea and I think the secret to really flavorful tea is to start with two bags of black tea leaves in a pre-heated pot. Pour boiling water over the tea leaves and let the pot steep for several minutes. It's never as full-bodied as coffee, but tolerable. Tea is nice for a dainty party or some frivolous occasion. It's especially good when my stomach isn't quite "right." I'm trying to convince myself that hot tea is good on a rainy afternoon. Any tea made with real tea leaves is a quantum leap ahead of herbal tea, which seems to me a lot like hot "Kool Ade." Deliver me from it.

Sometimes neither coffee nor tea will fit the bill. What I need is a glass of wine. Drinking wine is as much of an art as drinking coffee or tea. I pick up my glass and sniff the bouquet floating up from the surface of the wine and savor the aroma. The first small sip of wine livens up my taste buds. Then I feel the velvety smoothness of the wine slipping down my throat. Sipping slowly and gently, I enjoy every drop of that glass of wine. I prefer red wine, but blush or white wine will do.

Red wine with crackers and cheese is a great "happy hour" combination. Happy hour for us is a special time when my husband and I sit down together before dinner. That's life in a slower lane at its very best. One reason we enjoy it so much is that for many years while we were pursuing careers and raising a family, we had no time for such luxuries.

Now that I can savor wine during happy hour, I've developed some habits that would horrify true wine aficionados: I drink red wine with almost any entree. Red wine with pork has always been acceptable. Now that pork is the "other white meat," does it now call for white wine? Which wine is appropriate with salmon? It looks red enough to me to be called red meat. It's also a fatty fish and red wine seems to go well with other fatty entrees. Now that I rarely eat beef or any other really red meat, I'd never get any red wine without breaking some goofy gourmet rule. So I enjoy red wine and salmon together without a qualm. I haven't the least little pang of guilt because both are healthy choices.

Besides, it seems we can hardly eat or drink anything these days without getting the approval of a nutritionist and they don't always agree. Some say antioxidants in red wine slow aging, and omega-3 fatty acids in salmon and other cold-water fish help to fight heart and blood vessel disease. Some approve of modest alcohol consumption because they believe it wards off artery disease and reduces the risk of Alzheimer's disease and other dementias. I do hope I can hang on to at least one of these good reasons to drink red wine.

Coffee, tea, or wine–we sip each beverage and savor it at the same time we savor life in a slower lane.

Clean Sheets

Are you old enough to remember when everybody hung the laundry out to dry, usually on a Monday morning? In cities and towns people took pride in having their laundry out first or in having the whitest sheets. On the farm where I grew up there wasn't much competition because the clotheslines at one farm house were too far away from those at the next house to allow easy comparisons. Those were the "olden days" I guess, and only a few diehards like me still take pride in hanging laundry out.

Today most people toss sheets from the washer into the dryer and race on through a fast-paced day. Many have no place to hang laundry outdoors even if they had time to do it. I had a different slower-lane kind of day. I did the laundry and made the bed with clean sheets–not just any sheets, but sheets whipped dry in an early spring breeze, sheets that have billowed like the sails of a great ship. I wiped off the clotheslines and got out the clothespin bag I had brought in last fall. Preparing to hang the laundry outdoors is, for me, a kind of ritual of spring. It lifts my spirit. I like the idea of using solar energy in the form of sunlight and wind to dry the laundry.

When I bring the sheets in, they smell of fresh air. In a way, carrying sheets from the clothesline to the house is like bringing the outdoors indoors. Sure, they have tiny clothespin marks on their corners, but having those ever-so-fresh-smelling sheets makes such minor blemishes easy to take. I can't even see them when the lights are out and I'm lying in bed between those scrumptious sheets.

In addition to their fresh air aroma, outdoor dried sheets have a fluffed up texture all their own. They're not rough, not slick, they just have a special kind of smooth. In fact, I've often thought that line dried sheets are a special way to say to my family, "I love you." Stretching out to let those sheets caress my bare arms and legs is like lavishing love on myself. What a pleasure! Considering that such ecstasy came free of charge from the sun, it's got to be just about the cheapest luxury on earth.

From one laundry day to the next, the sheets loose their clothesline fresh aroma and their fluffy texture goes flat. But these qualities are easily renewed. All it takes is another trip through the washing machine and back on the line for another tussle with the wind and time in the sun. Wind-whipped sheets are great from spring to autumn, but the pleasure palls when cold sharp winds come and freeze the sheets to the line, stiff as a plywood plank. Before that happens I use the dryer to fluff those sheets and get on with my day like most everyone else.

Would that all aspects of life were as fresh and smooth and clean as sheets just in from the line. Alas, that's not the case. When I have a topsy-turvy day and things keep going wrong, I like to think metaphorically about clean sheets. If my writing goes awry, I want a clean sheet of paper. If I'm correcting mistakes in another part of my life, I speak of turning over a new leaf. I never willingly expose my problems or "hang my dirty laundry in public." I much prefer to solve my problems privately without fanfare or publicity. Literally or metaphorically, I like clean sheets.

On Sewing

Part of the joy of a slower-paced life is having the time and desire to reminisce about events that took place long ago. For me, one such event was learning to sew. Given the rough start I had with sewing, I'm still surprised that I ever came to enjoy it. Nonetheless, sewing has given me much pleasure over the years. When I make a garment, drapery, or slipcover, I have something to show for my efforts months or even years later. If I ever take the plunge into quilting, I might create heirlooms that would be cherished down through the generations. Other homemaking tasks don't last. When I clean house, it's dirty again in a few days. When I cook a meal, it's devoured, done for, in twenty minutes. Sewing lasts.

Back in the 1930s lots of people in the Midwest lacked electricity, so most women had treadle machines. Learning to use a treadle machine is a tricky business. It was a real ordeal in the otherwise carefree days of my childhood. The summer after I turned ten, I joined the 4-H Club and selected sewing as my first project. To complete my project I would need to hand-hem two tea towels and make either an apron or a slip. I chose the slip. It was not exactly the glamorous garment every young girl would pine for, but it was a serviceable addition to my wardrobe. I laid the pattern and cut out a front and a back piece. Mom showed me how to cut bias strips and sew them together. She said I would use those to bind the neck and armholes.

We went to the sewing machine. I had watched Mom operate the sewing machine many times—zoom, zoom, zoom—a seam was done, then another, and another. She made it look so easy that I thought learning to use the machine would be a snap.

"Here, you sit down in front of the machine," Mom said.

"Okay," I said as I sat down. Mom sat in a chair beside me and gave instructions.

"Take this sheet of paper and see if you can make the needle move right along a line. No, don't try to thread the machine. Not yet. That comes later."

I put the paper in place and started the needle at the end of a line. Then I tried to make the treadle go. The needle lurched forward, then backward, and finally stopped when I stopped pumping the treadle. I tried a dozen times with the same result before I got so I could keep the needle going up and down smoothly. The hard part was doing two things at once–keeping the needle on a line and managing the treadle so that the machine operated smoothly. If I didn't do it just right, the needle had another lurching fit. While I was trying to get the treadle under control, the needle would go off the line first to one side and then to the other. Coordinating everything was too much. I probably would have given up then and there, except that Mom didn't allow giving up, at least not the first afternoon. Eventually, with her patience and encouragement, I conquered the treadle and could make the needle come close to following the lines on the paper.

"Now, trade places with me and I'll show you how to thread the machine." I watched as Mom dragged the thread from the spool to the left, across the top of the machine, through a loop, down the front of the machine to a little gadget that regulates tension, back up to the top, down the right side and through every hook or loop along the way. Finally, Mom threaded the needle.

"Ready for me to sew now?" I asked.

"No, not 'til we get the bobbin in place. Watch while I wind a bobbin with white thread to match your slip." I watched but I didn't quite get it all.

"Don't go so fast," I said.

"Just get what you can. I'll go over this again when you need to do it." Mom finished putting the bobbin in place. "You come sit here. We'll make a side seam in your slip."

I put the cloth under the needle and made sure I didn't unthread the machine as I put the presser foot down. I started to sew. I couldn't keep track of everything and I let the cloth slither sideways. My seam was crooked.

"I give up," I said.

"No, you don't. You can do it. It just takes practice." Mom sat patiently beside me. She ripped out each crooked seam and handed the cloth back to me to try it again. I tried again and got it crooked again. Mom ripped and I sewed. Then I cried while she ripped. This went on all afternoon until I got two side seams more or less straight before I wore out the cloth. The short shoulder seams were much easier and I got them straight the first time. We saved the job of binding the armholes and neck for another day.

I finished the slip on another afternoon with fewer tears on my part and less ripping on Mom's part. The slip was soon ready to exhibit at the 4-H Fair in August. That garment lasted for years because I never wore it. I might have considered it a symbol of conquering the treadle and worn it proudly. But I didn't. I thought of it as two afternoons of tears, and I hated that slip. I still don't know how I came to like to sew after such a miserable start.

Sewing got easier over the years. For my second year 4-H project I made a dress from a floral print with a blue background. I even wore it now and then. The next year I found I could sew better than anybody else in my seventh grade home economics class. My friend, Carolyn, noticed my sewing and asked me to make her a vest. Then Dolores and Betty and Marietta wanted vests, too. I got so much practice with the treadle that I could make the sewing machine zoom along almost as well as Mom could.

One day when I was cleaning out the little drawers of the sewing machine cabinet, I found Mom's payment book for the machine. She had bought it the summer before I was born for $1 down and 25 cents a week. She must have really wanted that machine. She had recorded payments for only a few months and nowhere in the book did it say how much she paid for the machine. She must have paid it off early and left the payment book in the back of the drawer.

By the time I reached high school I made most of my clothes, that is, I remade hand-me-downs from my cousin, Ginny. One exception was a lined, wool gabardine suit I made from new cloth. That suit and I represented my county at the State Fair Dress Review. Alas, we didn't win a prize.

My successes with sewing and other 4-H projects netted me a full-tuition scholarship to Purdue, which at the time was worth $35 per semester. The scholarship was good only in home economics and I was interested in medicine. I accepted the scholarship anyway and enrolled in home economics courses. By the end of the first week of classes I knew that was a mistake. Every time the sewing class met, my eyes glazed over and my ears fogged up. An hour's demonstration on making and using bias tape was too much. Mom had taught me that when I was ten years old. By the end of the first semester I had gotten my fill of simple-minded instruction in sewing.

The next semester I forfeited my scholarship and became a biology major. Sewing had to be a sideline now that I had four or five science labs every week. When John and I became engaged, I asked my landlady if I could use her sewing machine to make my wedding dress.

"Can you use a treadle machine?" she asked.

"Sure can," I said proudly. She didn't need to know about the tears. The landlady had her old treadle machine moved into my room and I soon had my dress ready for the ceremony.

In the days of early marriage, homemaking, and babies, I made draperies, bedspreads, slipcovers, corduroy overalls in many sizes, nightgowns, pajamas, shorts and shirts for everyone, including my husband. When I was a stay-at-home mom riding herd on three pre-schoolers, I had lots of time to sew—at least a seam or two between interruptions.

I've always been glad Mom didn't let me quit before I learned to sew, and I tried to pass my skills on to my daughter and later to her two daughters. Each gave it a whirl, but none took any real interest, nor were they reduced to tears while trying. Do you suppose it takes a kind of trial by fire with lots of tears to make a person a dedicated seamstress?

The real test of a professed love of sewing is getting the mending done. Most people I know don't really like to mend things, but I like the challenge of making unobtrusive mends. I like the idea that for so little effort I can put garments back in service, wearable and looking nice. I suppose that's part of the "waste not, want not" motto we all lived by in my early years. Mending proved old adage, "A stitch in time saves nine."

Two things kept me sewing. First, I could make exactly what I wanted, and second, I could save bundles of money compared to the prices of equivalent ready-made items. For me, the joy of sewing is in the doing. Regardless of what I'm making, I get a little thrill out of seeing a new item take shape. Of course, I felt good about making my own wedding dress. I felt even better about making one for a granddaughter, but that's another story.

White Dress, Black Tux, and the Melding of Two Families

As I watched my husband escort our blonde granddaughter down the aisle toward the handsome, ebony-skinned love of her life, I think I was as ecstatic as the bride and groom themselves. I was happy that the antique satin dress I had made was a success. It had generously puffed sleeves, a sweetheart neck, and a three-layer tulle overskirt decorated with small satin bows. I was even happier that this biracial couple had the blessings of family and friends. Taunya and Aaron were such a radiant couple that I felt I might explode from my own exuberance.

I saw it all close up because I was already standing by my seat in a front pew. Being the family matriarch, I had been chosen to lead the wedding procession escorted by our son, Ed. Following Ed and me were the mothers of the bride and the groom, each with their own escorts. Then came the attendants, two pre-school age boys as ring-bearers, two slightly older flower girls, and at least five pairs of adult attendants, including our biracial granddaughter, Alexis, the maid of honor and sister of the bride. Creating the climax of the procession were the bride and her grandfather, moving in slow, stately steps. I didn't make a head count, but I think the wedding party and the guests were nearly perfectly balanced racially, half black and half white. All in all, a magnificent panoply and a beautiful wedding.

The ceremony got underway and everything proceeded according to plan. Well, almost. A minor delay occurred while the bride and groom stood with their backs to the guests, lighting a unity candle from candles lit by their mothers earlier in the ceremony. The delay morphed into an endearing moment when we later learned that the bride had gotten the "giggles." She soon regained her composure and the ceremony continued with no loss of dignity.

All too soon the magic moments passed. Aaron and Taunya, now husband and wife, walked down the aisle holding hands and beaming smiles in all directions. Taunya's sparkling blue eyes, translucent complexion, and her bouncy blonde curls made a glorious contrast with Aaron's flashing brown eyes and warm chocolate skin.

As we got to know Aaron, we found he fit right into the family as naturally as if he had been born into it. He had grown up in the south and must have suffered from all the prejudices and injustices one might expect. He moved to our nation's capital, worked his way through Howard University, and now has a promising career in computer science. It appeared to us that Aaron quickly felt at home with Taunya's family, especially her biracial sister, Alexis. We often laugh about his response to Alexis when one cold winter day she spoke of moving to the south where it was warm.

"No, Alexis," he said, "you've got it backwards. We're supposed to get out of the South, not go there."

Just as I volunteered to make a dress for the bride, I also offered to make one for granddaughter, Alexis. When the bridesmaids bought ready-made dresses and Alexis didn't need me to make hers, she asked if I would instead slipcover a couch someone had given her for her first apartment. Of course, I said I would. One day when I had way too much trouble with slippery, slithery satin, I wondered if I had taken on more than I could handle. But the wedding dress and the slipcover were more than ordinary commitments. They were labors of love for two cherished granddaughters. We always find ways to fulfill promises when they involve labors of love, don't we?

The logistics of these labors presented real challenges. With the granddaughters in Maryland and me in Pennsylvania, we met in the middle to shop for fabrics. I mailed a muslin bodice to the bride-to-be. A friend fitted it, and Taunya mailed it back. By

Thanksgiving, the dress was in three pieces: bodice, skirt, and tulle overskirt. John and I spent the holiday with our son Ric, daughter-in-law Jennifer, and grandson Cody, who also live in Maryland. While we were there, Jennifer generously volunteered to cater the wedding reception.

Aaron came for Thanksgiving dinner, but Taunya forbade his having the least little peek at the dress until their wedding day. I think she said that was supposed to bring bad luck. By Friday evening, the dress was finished and we were on our way back to Pennsylvania. Over the five weeks remaining before the wedding, we heard that Taunya's friends were worried she might wear the dress out trying it on to show all her friends, except, of course, her best friend Aaron.

With the dress finished, I started on the slipcover. I used cushions I had brought home as patterns and made three back and three seat cushion covers, all complete with zippers. But I needed to be in the same room with the sofa to finish the job. Back to Maryland we went toting my sewing machine, a card table, and some plastic chairs for Alexis' new apartment. By mid-afternoon the slipcover was done. We took Alexis out for a very late lunch and headed home.

I had never thought of slipcovers having anything to do with wedding dresses. Agreeing to a sewing task for each granddaughter was a matter of treating them fairly–not exactly alike, but according to their needs. Taunya didn't need a slipcover and Alexis didn't need a wedding dress, at least, not yet. (She once said that she wasn't going to get married, she was going to get a dog. We won't hold her to that.)

But back to the wedding. The celebration wasn't over until we all gathered for the reception and a lot of picture taking. Jennifer organized an amazing outlay of delicious treats for the reception. With some late night preparations and good help from Ric, Cody, and some of Taunya's friends, the food for the reception materialized as a magnificent coda to the wedding. Jennifer got requests for her catering services, but refused. She has another job and catered the reception just for a special niece.

All too soon, the white limousine arrived to transport the bride and groom away to the next phase of their lives together.

We were already to fete the pair with a rice-tossing farewell, but rice had been banned for ecological reasons. Once we understood, we didn't throw any dry rice for birds to glean in case it might swell in their crops and kill them. We happily accepted the substitute—individual bottles of soap bubble liquid and wands. We all gathered in front of the church and surrounded the couple with a flurry of bubbles as they descended the steps, climbed into the limousine, and were whisked away. Lots of people had worked together to make the day special for Taunya and Aaron. In the process they had also helped to lovingly meld two families together.

Rent-A-Pet and Callie's Response

Sometimes I'd like to rent a pet. I miss the days of my childhood when I nearly always had a dog and usually some barnyard cats, too. I miss the days when I was a young mother and our house was filled with children and dogs. Now that those children are grown and my husband and I are retired, we travel a lot and it's hard to find a good pet sitter or kennel. I really don't want to regularly walk a dog or serve daily cat box duty. What I really want is an occasional evening or two with a gentle, cuddly animal on my lap or snuggling beside me on the couch. A teddy bear won't do. I want a real live, warm, wiggly pet.

Why can't I rent a pet? Renting a pet seems like such a good idea for both pet lovers and pets that I can't imagine why I've never seen a kennel, veterinarian, or pet shop that offers a rental service. Such a service could increase human contact with a pet and improve the quality of care the pets receive. It would offer special pleasures for people who enjoy pets but who can't manage day-in-and-day-out responsibility for them.

Far too many pets live in homes where they are ignored or mistreated. They probably got plenty of attention and tender loving care when they were first adopted, but their keepers have lost interest. Now, if those keepers had rented their pets, they could have returned them when their enthusiasm waned. After a short hiatus, the pet would literally get a new lease on life.

Sometimes pet owners are intentionally cruel to their animals. If such people had rented their animals, the rental agent could check on their well being and repossess any animal that showed signs of mistreatment.

A kennel owner, veterinarian, or pet shop with extra boarding space could set up a Rent-A-Pet program with a small cadre of rental animals, maybe six dogs and six cats. The animals need not be pedigreed and could be mixed breeds from the animal shelter as long as they are healthy, neutered, immunized, and free of parasites. Dogs should be house-broken and cats box-trained. The pets should be young adult, medium-sized animals, no puppies, no kittens, and no large dogs that might be difficult to control. Some should be sturdy and placid enough to tolerate visiting families with small children. All rental animals must be consistently gentle and friendly.

Suppose I find a Rent-A-Pet shop and drop in.

"Good afternoon. May I help you," says the clerk.

"I hope you can. I'd like to rent a pet for the week end."

"Do you prefer a cat or a dog?"

"I think I'd like a cat this time. Do you provide litter boxes with your cats?"

"Of course, we do. We also provide food the animal is accustomed to and written instructions about how to care for each of our pets. May I show you the cats we have available?

"Yes, please." The clerk takes me to the cat room. I immediately take a liking to a little calico. "I'll take her," I say.

"She's a nice cuddly little cat. Her name is Callie," the clerk says.

The clerk puts the cat in a carrying cage and we all go back to the front of the shop. I pay the rent in full in advance and leave a security deposit. The clerk gives me a bag of food and goes over the sheet of instructions to be sure I understand and am able to comply. We're ready to go.

I get Callie home and show her where her litter box will be. She wanders around my place checking out all the new smells while I sit in my favorite living room chair waiting for her to make friends. Soon she comes and rubs against my legs. Next thing I know she's up in my lap, snuggled down and purring contentedly.

Had this been a real experience, Callie would have brought me much happiness. I can see how Rent-a-Pets could fill the lonely spots in the lives of many people, especially those who live alone. Many widows and widowers would benefit from a cat like Callie. A single man could enjoy having an energetic little dog greeting him at his door each evening for a week when he's home between business trips. A family with young children could find out whether their children are ready to take responsibility for a pet before they buy one. If this service were really available, a retired lady like me with a tolerant husband like mine could have a sweet little cat to curl up on her lap this evening. If I really could rent one, I'd go get it right now.

***

Had this been a real experience, Callie might have had a different view:

"Well, here I am back in the shelter. Am I being punished? What did I do wrong? The old lady that took me home with her was really nice to me. I thought she liked me and I liked her. I was all ready to settle into being her pet. It gave me quite a shock when she scooped me into a cage and took me back to the shelter. The really hard part was thinking I had found a home and somebody to love that would love me, too, then realizing it wasn't so. That made me so sad that I crawled into a corner of my cage and whined long into the night. I think I'm beginning to understand that I was only rented. Well, how would that lady like to be rented? How would she like not knowing when she might be evicted? I'd forgive her and give her another chance if she'd only come back and get me for keeps. I did like her."

Callie

The Re-Education of a WASP

Dignity hasn't always marked my family's handling of racial matters. Most of us simply knew nothing about other racial or ethnic groups. We were suspicious of anybody who wasn't just like us, and we responded with fear and rejection. Maybe that was a predictable response, but that didn't make it right. Maybe our ways of being discriminatory were neither vicious nor premeditated, but that didn't make them right either. My slower paced life these days gives me time to reflect on such matters.

In the 1930s the only black person in my home county was a live-in servant to a wealthy family. She almost never left the mansion. My Aunt Louise, who grew up in a city and married into our farm family, knew some of the more malignant city ways. She cautioned me to wash my hands after I handled coins. "They might have been on the eyelids of a dead 'darky," she said.

As I look back I realize that I grew up WASP. The term disgusts me now, but at the time I was surrounded by WASPS who thought themselves pure, white, and privileged. I was one of them by birth. We were anti-black, anti-Semitic, anti-Catholic, anti-anybody except white Protestants of acceptable ethnicity. We were so sure we did things right that we weren't even aware of our prejudices. We never discussed racial matters. That heavy silence told me that black people wouldn't be welcome in our county.

By the late 1940s when I was in high school, my mother, who taught elementary school music, was told to drop black-face minstrel shows from school musical performances. Town folk were outraged. They hadn't meant any harm and everybody enjoyed the show. I think this was my first glimmer of understanding of racial matters. I wondered why skin color mattered so much. Why not eye color or hair color? For example, if the privileged class had been blue-eyed blonds, then I and most of my family would have been the outcasts.

I went off to college in 1950 and began to meet different people–a black girl, among others. My black friend sat next to me in several classes and we sometimes walked across campus together. We usually talked about the class we had just attended. After that neither of us could think of anything to say. Our friendship never blossomed, probably because neither of us knew how to make a biracial friendship work. Before either of us figured out, a new semester came with a new class schedule. I lost track of my black friend.

When I married and my husband and I moved to San Antonio, we found ourselves part of a long-standing racial pecking order–whites on top, Hispanics in the middle, and blacks on the bottom. People seemed to know their places and I saw no outward signs of discontent. Their anguish about the inequalities and injustices of their lives must have boiled up inside them and made them hate white people. I'm sure it still does for many members of minorities.

I inadvertently made matters worse for a young black airman, who was my classmate at a local college. Some of my girlfriends and I were sitting at a lab table engaged in casual conversation.

"Look at my hair," I said to my friends.

"What about your hair?" one asked.

"Well, I put in a new home permanent yesterday, and now it looks like 'nigger fuzz,' that's what." Then I realized that the black airman had overheard my comment. He turned and walked away. I was humiliated, . . . mortified. My family had used that phrase when I was a child. I hadn't used it in years and I was sorely ashamed that it had spewed forth from my mouth. I never figured out how to apologize. Simply saying, "I'm sorry" would never have been enough.

By the time we moved to the Washington, D. C. area, the Civil Rights Movement was getting underway. A decade later I worked with a black man, who was on sabbatical leave from his position as dean of faculty in a predominantly black college. This John was the first black person I got to know really well. We once had a chat about whether it was harder to get ahead in science being a woman or being black. He thought women had a tougher time. I thought blacks did. We never resolved that issue.

One of John's special interests was in fostering creativity. Once he led a staff brainstorming session using a technique called "Synectics." One of the activities involved forming unlikely combinations of ideas, such as hypothetical two-word book titles–hot ice, happy grief, or moving statue. Working with John was a fascinating exercise in creative unpredictability.

Not long after I had formed that friendship, I was thrown into a real quandary. Our daughter started dating a black man, who had shown himself to be a violent man.

"Please don't get any further involved with that man," I said.

"He's dangerous," my husband added.

We couldn't explain why we thought the man was an inappropriate choice without sounding racist. He soon became the father of our second granddaughter.

For months before the birth of that child, I wondered what my reaction would be when I actually saw the child. The day came and I held that baby. I, the product of a WASP background, holding a biracial grandbaby in my arms. Awesome. How dare anyone hate my grandbaby! We now had two granddaughters, one blonde and one biracial.

The years passed and we weathered storms, but we all tried to keep communication open. Sometimes we felt we were picking our way through a mine field. Our granddaughters grew to adulthood all too soon, and as a family we came through our experiences stronger and more compassionate. When the blonde granddaughter announced plans for a biracial wedding, we were anxious to get acquainted with the groom. One surprising thing we learned was that he had never known either of his grandfathers.

At the wedding, the bride in a white satin dress and the groom in a black tuxedo, stood together as a living symbol of racial unity. A few weeks after the wedding, the young couple came to visit us for a weekend. The groom wanted particularly to get better acquainted with his new grandfather. Since that time both grandfather and grandson have thrived in their relationship, and this old, one-time WASP has rejoiced in her biracial family.

On Grandmothering

Grandmothering takes some special talents. Now that I have more than twenty years of experience as a grandmother, I know that. A grandmother must polish skills she learned long before they were called grandparenting skills. She must give generously of time and ration gifts prudently lest the children become too mercenary about Grandma. To cement a grandmother-grandchild relationship, a grandmother must offer up a big dollop of special attention and caring, what some people call "spoiling." Such attention probably would be spoiling if parents did it, but grandmothers are supposed to do it. They can get by with it. Grandmas and kids love it.

I got an early start at learning grandmothering skills when I stayed with my maternal grandmother at the old family farmhouse while my mother taught school. In fact, I know from family lore that my grandmother was standing by the bedside while I was being born. She must have been the first person to hold me. From that time on, I was "the apple of her eye." At least that's what I always thought. Grandma and I shared the doting on my little brother who came when I was ten. I could never have accepted the idea that he had replaced me as Grandma's "apple." I'm not sure how Grandma pulled it off, but somehow she made me feel I was her grown-up ally and helpmate in caring for him.

I don't suppose Grandma was perfect in all respects, but she certainly had that grandmothering thing down pat. She listened to my every word as I followed her around, prattling all day long. I've never figured out how she could listen patiently for so long. I'm sure I would have told a child, "Hush and go find something to do." Grandma didn't do that. She dried my tears and held me when I was hurt or scared. When I was sick, which wasn't very often, she put a cold cloth on my feverish brow and made me some milk toast, my family's favorite "sick person" food. Any grandmother who doesn't know how to make milk toast needs a lesson now. It's simple. You just toast and butter a slice of bread and lay it in a shallow bowl. Then heat about half a cup of milk and pour it over the toast. Offered with tenderness by a grandmother, it always makes a sick child feel better. At least it did in my family.

My wish was not always Grandma's command. She didn't let me do as I pleased all the time. I had some boundaries like the fence around the yard.

"Stay inside the fence," Grandmother would say. "Men working there with machinery or animals won't be looking out for a little girl. You could get hurt."

"Okay," I answered cheerfully. I took Grandma's word for these things and didn't even test them. The gospel according to Grandma was good enough for me.

Grandma didn't cater to my every whim either.

"Read me a story, Grandma." I said..

"After I finish what I'm doing," she answered.

I had to wait until she ironed a shirt, finished washing dishes, or put cake batter in pans and into the oven, but I always knew she would keep her promise.

I don't remember this grandmother giving me birthday or Christmas gifts. She had no money except for what she made selling eggs. But she made me feel like I was her partner in whatever work we were doing. I wasn't just a little kid. I was an important and valuable member of the family. Grandma gave me some of life's priceless things.

This grandmother's greatest failing was her inability to stand up to the overbearing demeanor of strong-willed family members. She caved in every time her sister-in-law demanded something ridiculous, like congealed oatmeal.

I stood in awe one Sunday morning when I was about ten and my Uncle Frank took over the task of making Aunt Nett's oatmeal. When he finished, he said, "Here's your damned oatmeal made exactly by the directions on the package. Now sit down and eat it."

She sat and ate without further ado. Had Grandma done the same kind of thing, she could have saved herself years of being the victim of family bullies. Grandma continued to wait on family members. She fixed their meals, did their laundry, and kept their rooms clean. They took it as their due and Grandma obliged. She did almost anything to avoid family strife. It made me very angry to see how Grandma was "walked on" by demanding relatives. Thinking about it sixty years later, it still makes me angry.

I saw less of my paternal grandmother because my father and mother were divorced. Even so, my mother made sure I got to visit that grandmother often, usually on a Saturday. I always found Grandma pottering in the kitchen. Like my other grandmother, she always had time to let me help her. Cinnamon pastries were my specialty at her house. Standing by watching a three-year-old roll out pastry scraps and spread them with sugar and cinnamon must have taken a great deal of patience and she had it. In fact, I think she made a pie when she knew Mom was bringing me so she would have pastry scraps for me to play with. I wish I had seen more of her. I'm sure she had more stories to tell and more cuddling to do.

My own mother was less obliging than my grandmothers. She never took advantage of her mother, but she let people know if she felt they were taking advantage of her. She was strict with me, but she was much more lenient as the grandmother of my children. For several summers, my children went, one at a time, to spend a week with her. During those special weeks, she provided special treats for the honored grandchild–a trip to the small town of Santa Claus, Indiana, a pony ride, or a swim in a nearby pool. She taught the children card games and never ran out of patience playing with them. Also, she always took them shopping for clothes that both they and their grandmother liked.

We had all heard my mother talk about the pony and cart she had as a little girl. Once she bought a new pony and cart "to give the grandkids rides," she said. I think she also enjoyed re-living a piece of her own childhood. The particular pony she got was a grave disappointment because he startled easily. One time when Mom had our daughter and my brother's two boys, ages two and five, in the cart with her, a car sped past. The pony ran down an embankment and dumped the cart and passengers in a field of wheat stubble. Mom had some broken ribs but the children weren't seriously injured. Our daughter, Diane, spent a good part of her week with Grandma taking care of the cousins while the ribs began to heal. Diane liked caring for her cousins. The five-year-old cousin summed up the accident tersely, "Damned near killed us all."

By the time my mother became a great-grandmother, she was officially living in her own slower lane and could lavish time on her two great granddaughters. When we visited, Mom always served something good to eat. Then she started a favorite card game called "Thirty-One"and played as long as the girls were interested. Later during the visit, she took them shopping. They idolized her.

These grandmothers gave me a hard act to follow. Some day I'll get to see how my daughter fares as a grandmother and a great-grandmother. I think we'll do fine.

On Mothering

Mothering is harder for me to write about than grandmothering. I've had more experience mothering, but I had a different relationship with my mother than with either grandmother. I always trusted Mom because she was self-confident and dependable. She could step in and keep the post office running smoothly when her aunt, the postmaster, couldn't work. She could run the family insurance agency without a hitch. When there was plowing, planting, or cultivating to do on the farm, Mom could hop on the tractor and do the job as well as any man. I don't remember seeing her drive a team of horses, but I've been told by other members of the family that she could handle that, too. She always seemed to know what to do in any situation. All of Mom's friends counted on her.

It was long after I became a mother that people began talking about role models. That was when I realized my Mom had been a remarkable role model for me when I was a young girl developing self-confidence and dependability. I always took it as a compliment when someone said I was just like my mother.

When I was in elementary school, Mom always taught one of the grades. She always seemed to be in control in her classroom. Because our small school had only one teacher and one room for each grade, it was inevitable that some year I would be in Mom's class. It happened in third grade. Mom treated me like any other student in the class, except when it came to making allowances for occasional lapses in performance, such as careless spelling or math errors. Some students got the benefit of the doubt. I never did. No one could ever accuse Mom of showing favoritism toward me. She abhorred the idea of any person getting special privileges, and she inculcated that viewpoint in me. I would have been ashamed to receive any special treatment.

My best memories of my mother come from times we worked together on various projects. She genuinely appreciated my accomplishments. In the summertime we worked together along with Grandma to plant, cultivate, and harvest the garden. We canned and froze vegetables. In those days we rented frozen food storage lockers in a central building about four miles from home. Mom elected me to stow the boxed foods in summer and to retrieve whatever she needed for the week every Saturday morning during the rest of the year.

"Get two chickens, three boxes of green beans, two boxes each of limas and corn, and a box of peaches," she said.

"Got it," I answered as I grabbed my jacket and headed for the cold room.

We also worked together painting things, usually rooms in the house. One summer we painted a small barn behind the house. The challenge was to climb a twenty-foot extension ladder to reach the siding at the peak of the roof.

"Who's going up the ladder?" I asked.

"I though you could do that," she said.

"That'll be fun."

We were a good team no matter whether we were making garden, painting a barn, or doing some other chores. Nonetheless, sometimes Mom got upset with me. She had a certain look she gave me, a penetrating stare with her steely black eyes. It felt like she could see right inside my head and know what I was thinking. She never yelled at me, in fact, she didn't even scold. She didn't need to. She just gave me the "look." That look was handed down from Mom to my daughter, Diane, skipping me. I realized Diane had the same talent when I heard one of her grown daughters jokingly ask just this past weekend, "Mom, what happened to the "look?"

My mother always gave the impression that she knew exactly what she wanted to accomplish and was sure she could do it. If she had doubts, she kept them to herself. She also had an innate sense of how to help a child develop self-confidence. She did it by displaying as much confidence in her students as she had in herself.

One year the superintendent wanted to place Jackie, a severely retarded child, in a classroom so he could experience being with other children. There were no special education classes back in the 1940s, at least not in rural Indiana.

"We can't do anything for him," some teachers said.

Others said, "He'll disrupt the class and keep other children from learning."

Mom said, "I'll take him. Put him in my class."

When Mom tried to teach Jackie to read, she soon discovered that he couldn't manage it. Then she taught him to make hooked rugs. The other children sometimes stopped by his desk to watch him work. I think some were a little envious of the beautiful work Jackie did. For the first time, Jackie had a skill he could be proud of. Having his teacher praise his beautiful work was icing on the cake.

With all her ambition, Mom had to live with disappointment, too. For one thing, she was terribly disappointed that I had almost no musical talent.

When I was seven years old and finishing first grade, Mom asked, "Would you like to learn to play the piano?"

"Yes, yes," I danced with excitement.

Mom bought a piano and arranged for me to take lessons. I made slow progress, but she kept paying for lessons year after year. When I started junior high school, I wanted a clarinet so I could play in the band. Mom bought a clarinet and arranged both piano and clarinet lessons. In high school, I wanted a saxophone. Mom got that, too, and paid for more lessons. Throughout all those years of lessons, I claimed I really wanted to learn. Mom never gave up the hope that I would someday catch on. I never did.

***

Not long ago I read a book entitled *Mother Nature* by S. B. Hrdy that gave me a broad perspective on mothering and the assurance that some of my intuitions were correct. First, it taught me to be thankful for the stability my family provided as I was growing up. In spite of the fact that my parents were divorced, I never felt deprived or insecure. Second, I realized that many very young mothers are unable to cope with motherhood. That made me even more grateful for the mature mother I had.

Third, Hrdy explained how generations of women who depended on breast-feeding succeeded by letting their babies nurse anytime they acted hungry. Every mother in my family, up to and including my mother, breast-fed their babies. None of the rest of us have succeeded for several reasons. Alternative food is readily available. For many years doctors encouraged schedules for babies. And most importantly, nobody fully understand the importance of really frequent, prolonged suckling to stimulate a steady supply of milk.

Fourth, Hrdy emphasized the importance of family. She notes that when fathers are not available, grandfathers and uncles tend to reduce the economic and psychological stresses to which children are subjected. My step-father and my mother's brother filled that gap in my life.

Finally, Hrdy noted that grandmothers and other older females have routinely helped young mothers. That was true for me and my daughter, and it would have been true for my mother and me if I had lived close to her. Apparently, it's generally true from foraging primates to modern-day human mothers.

***

For all my efforts to reflect on mothering and being mothered, I find it very difficult to say what kind of mother I was. I tried to follow some of my mother's practices and some of my grandmother's. Too often I got frustrated and yelled at my children, and I can't say I learned that from either Mom or Grandma. I think if my children were to read what I've written, they would probably say, "You were more tolerant but also a little more wishy-washy and less consistent than your Mom."

From Fear to Speaking Out

It's taken years to learn to talk about it, but I'll tell you now: I'm the mother of a gay son. That knowledge filled me with fear for our whole family, my husband John, myself, and our four children, ages ten to twenty. We got word of our fate on a spring Saturday in the mid-1970s, in our modest, brick colonial home in a Washington, D. C. suburb. John and I were alone when one of our son Ed's closest friends came to break the news that 16-year-old Ed was gay. The friend could see we were shocked and he didn't stay long. After he left, we sat down to talk.

"John," I said, "I don't believe it."

"I just don't know," he answered.

"What should we do? Talk to Ed about it? What?"

"Maybe if we wait, he'll tell us himself."

While we waited, I worried that if word got out about our gay son, friends and maybe family would reject us. At the same time, I wanted to hug that son and say, "It's okay." But I didn't know how. For weeks we didn't talk about gayness, hoping, I guess, that if we ignored it, it would go away. It didn't. It sat at the dinner table with us. It followed us wherever we went. It came to bed with us and woke us up in the night. We simply had to address that ever-present, paralyzing ghost. We had to learn to talk about homosexuality.

Talk we did one Sunday evening when Ed lingered in the living room. I don't recall who broke the ice, but I remember that Ed told us in his own words that he was gay.

"What Skip told you is true. I am gay."

"That's okay," I said.

"Yes," John said, "we love you no matter what."

"But are you really sure?" I couldn't help asking.

"Yes, I broke up with my girlfriend because I had fantasies about fellows when I was with her. I thought that wasn't fair to her. I would have told you sooner, but I didn't want to hurt you."

And we wanted to ask but we didn't want to hurt you."

"Isn't that ironic, everybody hurting each other by trying not to hurt each other," Ed said.

"Yes," we agreed. We all felt much relieved and ended our conversation with hugs all around. We had managed the hardest part—that first conversation.

As a family we struggled to stay connected and to protect ourselves against a cold, unwelcoming outside world. The consequences if people discovered Ed was gay were terrifying. People might ostracize him before his peers. Gay bashers might injure him. I wanted to protect my gay son, but I didn't know how. I feared that whispered words behind our backs could undermine acceptance for all of us. I felt helpless.

Our conversation with Ed set me thinking back to 1949 when I was sixteen and had never known a gay or lesbian person, that is, I had never known anyone who openly declared his or her homosexuality. Nobody I knew even mentioned homosexuality, but somehow I sensed that it was bad. Now I had to change my views to fit the kind of person I knew my son to be–a kind, loving, and loveable young man. Eventually I cast away old notions and learned to respect sexual orientation as an important part of every person's core of being, including that of our gay son.

Wanting to do something positive, I began seeking information about homosexuality and found more questions than answers. In the 1970s the American Psychiatric Association still classified homosexuality as a mental illness and prescribed counseling and electroshock therapy. My gut feeling told me that couldn't be right, and my psychologist husband agreed. Eventually, the Association changed its views. I read about families who disowned gay and lesbian children, literally kicked them out of the house. While I felt a deep sadness for these children and their families, I took some much-needed solace in the fact that our family was maintaining fragile lifelines of communication.

No matter how much reading I did, I still had questions. How could I have a gay son? How could this happen to our family? Did I do something wrong as a mother? Was anything really wrong? The most accepted explanation for male homosexuality in the 1970s was that domineering mothers caused their sons to be gay. Ouch! I had to admit that I was a confident person with a forceful personality. Was I domineering enough to make my son gay? Then how come only one of my three sons was gay? I absolved myself from that guilt, but mothers who accepted it must have carried a terrible and undeserved burden.

I turned next to my own field, biology, for answers. Was a genetic factor involved? To consider that, I needed to know if any of my husband's or my living relatives or ancestors were gay or lesbian. If I lacked the courage to ask living family members, I couldn't expect that people in earlier generations had spoken of homosexuality. Nobody knew what caused homosexuality. Given the dark cloak of secrecy around the topic, nobody was likely to learn.

Over the next decade as our children grew to adulthood, homosexuality became less of a hush-hush subject. Nonetheless, we were still careful what we said and where we talked about homosexuality. Only after I marched with women in an Equal Rights Demonstration on the Washington Mall did I learn that Ed had marched with a group of gays. By his participation Ed publicly acknowledged his homosexuality. I was glad that we had both participated, but I worried that Ed might be risking victimization by gay-bashers.

By 1992 my husband and I had retired and moved to a college town in Pennsylvania, where we joined the local Unitarian Universalist Fellowship. We soon learned that the minister had performed a ceremony of union for a same-sex couple. I had read about such ceremonies, but now I was part of a community that accepted them. I soon came to cherish the Fellowship as a safe place to speak out about our gay son.

We also joined the local chapter of Parents, Families, and Friends of Lesbians and Gays (PFLAG). Among sympathetic listeners, I mustered the courage to "come out" as a spokesperson for gay and lesbian rights. I wasn't so brave among religious conservatives who believed homosexuality was a sin and repentance its remedy. I knew we must not condone unjust treatment of homosexuals, but I lacked the courage to speak out in the wider community. Then a UU friend with a soft, gentle voice showed me how to grow that courage. "Joan," she said, "we cannot stand by and let derogatory comments go unchallenged. We must speak out against unfair accusations, prejudice, and violence." At the time she worked with battered women, but she made me see that speaking out for the causes of gays required the same kind of courage. Her words strengthened my resolve. If she could speak out, so could I.

At PFLAG meetings I learned about the kinds of experiences gays and lesbians must endure. I was appalled to learn that taunts like "faggot" were among the lesser humiliations. My understanding grew and so did my courage. I was surprised to learn that homosexuals seemed to know at what age they recognized their own sexual orientation, but heterosexuals did not. The latter claimed they had always been heterosexual and that everybody was born heterosexual. Then they concluded from their erroneous assumptions that gays and lesbians must have chosen to be homosexual.

One lesbian countered by saying, "Considering rejection, hatred, and the risk of becoming a victim of gay-bashing that homosexuals suffer, why would anyone *choose* to be gay or lesbian?" Many PFLAG members reported painful struggles to be like their "straight" peers. A particularly forthright lesbian, now a strong supporter of PFLAG, told how as a teenager her overwhelming need to belong had led her to participate in gay bashing. "I so needed to be part of the 'in-group' that I couldn't admit even to myself that I was a lesbian. Even after I accepted my own identity, I didn't dare admit it to any of my friends. But I did stop participating in the bashings."

Bashings, suicides, and AIDS are frequent causes of death among homosexuals. The bashing of Matthew Shepard led to murder when he was tied to a fence, beaten, and left to die alone. The agony of rejection leads many gays and lesbians to commit suicide. Parents find a heart-wrenching note next to their dead child, "Dear Mom and Dad, The torment was too great. I just couldn't go on. I love you." Until recently, AIDS delivered a certain death sentence. Now medications prolong the lives of infected individuals who can afford them. Drugs came too late for Ed's closest childhood friend who met an untimely death from AIDS. We all mourned him.

All my experiences—UU and PFLAG programs, hearing about suicides, grieving an AIDS death—came together to strengthen my courage. Three acquaintances unwittingly gave me opportunities to use it.

First, a friend and I were discussing the possibility of going to a convention.

"I don't want to go to that convention because it's full of gays," she said.

"Oh," I answered. "It disturbs me to hear you say that because I have a gay son."

After a long, awkward silence, my friend said, "Oh, er, I didn't mean anything by that. I have nothing against, er, er, those people."

Then a retired pediatrician, lamenting the state of society, said, "If it weren't for all those gays and pedophiles, . . .

"Oh, dear, I'm sorry you feel that way. Did you know we have a gay son?"

"Ah, er, no," said the doctor, and he managed an awkward apology.

Finally, I was involved in a discussion about homosexuality within my own Unitarian community when one lady said of gays and lesbians, "I just wish they'd go away." The rest of us just stared at her, not knowing what to say. I think the shocked looks on our faces spoke more eloquently than words.

When I confront people who make negative comments about homosexuals, I usually ask whether they know any gays or lesbians. Most admit that they do not. Given that about one in ten Americans is homosexual, most people probably know several without knowing their sexual orientations. A friend of mine explained, "Of course they don't know any gays. Their disrespectful views precede them and no gays will be known to them."

I think that in the interests of justice, we must gather the courage to speak out and help eradicate anti-gay attitudes from our culture. We can speak gently. We can raise questions. We can politely call attention to offensive statements. We can particularize our comments with references to people we know– "my gay son" or "my lesbian friend." Speak out we must, even when it embarrasses someone or elicits a barrage of verbal backpedaling. Such situations are uncomfortable, but they challenge offenders to reconsider their views. On a broader front, we must work together to hold public officials and institutions accountable. We must pressure them to enact and enforce laws that honor the civil rights of every citizen.

As I reflect on experiences with my gay son, I think it's a miracle that he and many others like him remain tolerant, loving people in spite of physical and verbal abuse from a society that maligns and rebukes them at every turn. Even though there is no accepted explanation of how sexual orientation develops, I know my son didn't choose his homosexuality any more than I chose my heterosexuality. We all deserve the same rights and privileges, regardless of sexual orientation--the right to form legal domestic unions, to be with our partners during illnesses, to enjoy the same employment opportunities and benefits, and to be treated with dignity and respect.

I'm tired of hearing the morally righteous speak about protecting their families from homosexuals. When will they use their righteousness to support justice for all? When will they help to protect my gay son and other gays and lesbians from those who would abuse them? When will we all work together to dispel fears and replace hatred with compassion? When will we respect the dignity of every person, including my son and other homosexual sons and daughters? I'll know we're finally home free when everyone thinks of sexual orientation as one of many personal attributes like blue eyes, curly hair, brown skin, sunny or crotchety disposition that make a person who she or he is. That's how I look at my gay son. I accept him just the way he is. Above all, I love and honor him for who he is.

Moving-In Day

Every year at the end of summer, college campuses across America celebrate Moving-In Day, or rather a long weekend of moving-in days. In the college town where we chose to retire, I try to stay out of the way of moving-in days. Nonetheless, any errand that takes me along the perimeter of the campus gives me a view of the process. I can't help noticing the multitude of things students bring with them–books, clothes, and a computer, of course. Many also bring an extra bookcase, a stereo, a microwave, a TV, and, if possible, a car. Traffic jams at the big box stores attest to students' needs for drapes, bedspreads, carpet, bulletin boards, sundry school supplies, posters, pennants, and wastebaskets. Articles emblazoned with the college logo are best sellers. When I see them in stores, I can't help wondering how all the Janes, Jills, Jacks, and Joes tell their wastebaskets apart. Indeed, whatever happened to individuality?

Back at the dorms, every sidewalk is littered with disheartening displays of rampant materialism. Parents and siblings unload carton after carton from the back of the family's new SUV, itself a machine of environmental devastation. On average, students import about ten "plug-in" possessions each–hair dryers, curling irons, shavers, desk lamps, pencil sharpeners, clothes irons. They even bring heating pads in anticipation of sports injuries.

I fear the world simply lacks sufficient raw materials for everyone to have as much "stuff" as today's students bring to college. Insurance companies caution parents to be sure they have sufficient coverage for all the loot they help their kids transport on moving-in day. Some colleges actually encourage students to bring their own computers and they vow to provide "one port per pillow" in dorm rooms.

The most shocking statistic is that of the nation's two million college students, one-third to one-half own a halogen torcherie. That's literally the hottest lamp in town—300 to 500 watts! Such lamps have caused nearly two hundred fires and eleven deaths. Some colleges ban them. One college I read about swaps them for fluorescent desk lamps. I would guess that a particular college may have stockpiled as many as five thousand confiscated torcheries–enough to light, or perhaps set alight, the football stadium.

I must live in a different, slower paced world because I've never owned a torcherie. I'm trying to simplify my life while the students seem to be laboring mightily to complicate theirs. Even so, I'll never again be able to make my life as simple as it was when I first went off to college over fifty years ago with two suitcases, a box of books, and a portable typewriter. Nor will my husband and I return to the time when we wedged all our worldly possessions into a second-hand Chevy, said our marriage vows, and set out for his new job in Texas.

We are, nonetheless, divesting ourselves of possessions we don't need. We recently sold our thirteen-year-old, beloved Chevy Nova to a local cab company, and left the lot feeling like we had parted with a member of our family. I'm sure that when I see a certain dark blue taxi, I'll want to give it a pat on its little ol' hatch back and hope it's faithfully serving its new master.

We're also trying to recycle everything we can, but the students we observe don't seem to be recycling much of anything. Most of the things I saw hanging out of vans and SUVs or standing in pick-up trucks were so new they hadn't left their original packing cases. Surely, some students arrive with well-worn possessions in a not-so-new passenger car, the collegiate equivalent of a plain brown wrapper. I couldn't see them for all the stuff that blocked my view.

I wonder when students will start to curb their consumptive habits and simplify their lives. Probably not until they learn to measure self-worth in personal accomplishments instead of the volume and cost of their possessions, and that will take a while. I also wonder how they will ever manage to study with all the distractions they provide for themselves. Some will and some won't, of course. And by the end of the semester we'll know which are which.

On Driving

Like many seniors today, I learned to drive at a time when there was relatively little traffic, speeds were lower, and the risks of bodily harm were smaller. Looking back, it seems as if we were born to life in a slower lane, but that's not entirely true. On the farm where I grew up, we worked hard and we managed without most of today's labor saving aids. We looked like we were in the slow lane because it took longer to get things done, not because we had much leisure.

I actually learned to drive on a tractor in a forty-acre pasture when I was about fourteen years old. That tantalizing taste of "having wheels" set me pining for a driver's license and the freedom of the road. Before I reached the magic age of 16 and eligibility for a license, my great aunt became partially crippled with some undiagnosed paralysis, probably a small stroke and needed a chauffeur. I was more than willing to oblige. Mom couldn't leave work just any old time to taxi her aunt so she had to either risk letting her aunt drive or let me be the chauffeur. She chose the risk of my getting stopped without a driver's license for the remaining few months until I got my license. The year was 1948 and the place was rural southern Indiana–not exactly a high risk traffic area. So, at age fifteen, I drove my great aunt from our farm on the edge of town to wherever she needed to go and came directly back to the farm. I did most of my driving during the summer. While school was in session I usually drove early in the morning or after school.

Being Aunt Nett's chauffeur wasn't exactly the freedom of the road I longed for. I couldn't go where I wanted to go, only where my aunt wanted to go, and she wanted to go to some pretty dull places–her insurance agency or the post office. Our most exciting trips involved driving out in the country to inspect the barn roof for somebody who wanted to buy insurance. I chauffeured my aunt for nearly a year without a license and never got stopped. Neither did I ever strike out for an unauthorized destination. I knew somebody would see me and tell Mom where they saw me. In our small community where everybody knew everybody else and their business, Mom would have heard about my transgression before I got home. And I was much more afraid of Mom's disapproving stare than I was of any policeman I'd ever seen.

With all that driving experience under my belt, I finally got a learner's permit a few months before my birthday as dictated by state law. Mom or Dad spent some time riding with me so I could officially learn to drive. I nearly flunked Dad's test one Saturday afternoon when we were approaching a bridge over a creek. This particular bridge had crosswise boards for the bridge deck and two lengthwise strips where tires could run more smoothly if the driver could keep the car on the strips. I stopped and looked at Dad. He didn't say anything. He just sat there with a funny little grin on his face. Eventually I got the message that if I was going to learn to drive I had to learn to drive across that bridge. I drove across without incident.

My sixteenth birthday happened to fall on the one day of the week that the only licensing agency in our county was open. I took the test and got my license that very day. I've been driving ever since, and I still like to drive. After I got a license, I didn't worry about what vehicle I would drive. I just assumed that Mom, Dad, or somebody would happily lend me a vehicle when I want to go someplace. Most of the time someone did.

Soon after I got my license, Aunt Nett fell and broke her hip, or more probably, her old, brittle hip broke and she fell. She was taken by ambulance to a hospital forty miles from home. This gave me an opportunity to make some of the trips to the hospital each week to check on her and keep her company.

A year later, I went off to college and found myself on foot again, this time on a sprawling campus. Once in a while Mom let me take her car back to campus for a week, but it was a real hardship for her and I knew it. I didn't ask often.

At the end of my second year of college, John and I got married and bought a second-hand Chevy to take us to Texas, where John had a job lined up. We shared the driving on that thousand mile trip, the longest trip I had ever taken. After that long trek, I still loved driving and the heady feeling I got from driving our own car.

Since that time I have driven in every one of the fifty states and all Canadian provinces. I've driven a rental car in Europe and in Israel, Fiji, Australia, and New Zealand. My first experience with driving on the left side of the road was in Fiji, where there wasn't much traffic. Having little traffic isn't always good because observing the flow of traffic is a reminder to pull into the proper lane when entering a road. Another trouble spot is watching for oncoming traffic when making a right turn. Back home it's canceling new habits and watching for incoming traffic when making a left turn. We had a rustic, but cozy, mini-camper for most of the 1990s. We made several nice trips in the American west, Great Lakes, and Canadian maritime provinces. I still miss it.

Why do I like to drive? Please believe me when I say it is not power mania. I think it's a combination of being free of responsibilities at home and being on my way to some interesting place. Anticipation of what I might see along the way and at my destination thrills me to the core. I like traveling by car better than by public transportation because a car offers flexibility for tailoring a trip to our particular whims. We stop where we want, stay as long as we want, and go as far as we want. When we had a small camper, we could simply pull over when we were ready for a meal or needed to use our bathroom. That was the ultimate in flexibility, and flexibility is important to me.

We've taken a few trips by bus and train. Formal tours are my least favorite way to travel because I must stop where the tour stops, and I miss many wonderful photo opportunities that weren't located at scheduled stops. Traveling by tour bus meant we waited patiently if not cheerfully for gift shop lollygaggers, and impatiently for inconsiderate stragglers to board the bus in the morning, drag themselves and their packages onto the bus after stops, and otherwise inconvenience everyone except themselves. We like train travel, especially in Europe and Canada. Seats are roomy and comfortable and the tracks often pass through magnificent scenery not visible from any road. One drawback is the acrobatic talents required to get into and out of upper berths.

Back to traveling by car, I like moving through space, not high above the clouds, but close to the ground and at a speed that lets me enjoy the scenery. Nobody knows exactly where I am, and I like that feeling, too. My husband and I can take in all the scenic overlooks. We can seek out the two-lane, tree-lined back roads. I absolutely adore driving steep, narrow, winding mountain roads. Whenever I find any of these attractive environs bedecked with a layer of fresh snow, I'm beside myself with joy. I think I'll never stay home as long as I can go, especially if I can drive.

Now that many of us are concerned about our environment–air pollution and global warming caused by the burning of fossil fuels–I have some pangs of guilt about being responsible for my contribution to those problems. I salve my conscience with the fact that we have only one car and for most of the year we put ten gallons of gas in our tank only once every two weeks. No matter how old I get, as long as I'm a safe driver and I can get fuel for a small car, just leave the driving to me.

The Icarus Syndrome

The summer of 2001 was a long, hot summer here in Pennsylvania. High temperatures in July soared five degrees above the average highs and higher yet in August. Breezes were rare and tree leaves hung paralyzed in the heavy, humid air. As I looked up toward the hazy sky, I thought of the Greek myth about Icarus and his father Daedalus.

According to the myth, both father and son got stranded in the labyrinth of King Minos on the Isle of Crete. Daedalus devised a plan to free them. They would build wings of feathers, attach them with wax, and fly the seventy miles across water from Crete to the mainland of Greece. As they departed, Daedalus cautioned Icarus not to fly too close to the sun lest it melt the wax that held his wings on. Brash young Icarus, giddy with the power of flight, soared higher and higher until his wings fell off and he plunged to his death.

Yes, I thought, as I headed for a shady spot, we Americans suffer from the Icarus Syndrome. We seem to think that we can continue to lead the world in fossil fuel use and that warnings about global warming don't apply to us. But they do. Although global warming was almost unheard of a decade ago, we now have ample evidence that it is real. And we know that it is caused mainly by burning fossil fuels that release carbon dioxide into the atmosphere. The carbon dioxide forms a kind of blanket that traps heat near the earth's surface. Without that heat our planet would be too cold for living things to thrive, but too much heat can also threaten our survival.

Before the Industrial Revolution, carbon dioxide made up 0.028 percent of the atmosphere, but now it makes up 0.036

percent. That amount of carbon dioxide may seem negligible, but it actually amounts to a 30 percent increase.

We've already seen some effects of global warming–melting glaciers, increases in sea level, and salt-water encroachment in low-lying areas. Melting glaciers have caused sea levels to rise 10 to 25 centimeters (4 to 10 inches) in the last century. More recently in the summer of 1998, Bangladesh experienced significant flooding that drove people from their homes, destroyed farmland, and caused salt infiltration into freshwater reservoirs. It also led to microbial contamination of water supplies. Some other low-lying areas presently vulnerable to these threats are closer to home–New Orleans, Houston, and Miami. The Bahamas, Venice, Italy, and coastal areas of the Netherlands are also threatened.

A closer look at the New Orleans area shows that for the past several years, 35 square miles of wetlands in southern Louisiana have sunk into the Gulf of Mexico each year. Thirty-five square miles is equivalent to the land area occupied by a small city, such as Rochester, New York or Colorado Springs, Colorado. Wetlands may look like worthless swamps, but they are, in fact, extremely valuable "nurseries"that protect the young of various species until they can fend for themselves in open water. Forty percent of the total U. S. fish and seafood catch starts out in these wetlands. Louisiana's portion of our nation's fishing industry is a $2 billion a year business.

So far, southern Louisiana has been lucky to avoid the direct hit of a hurricane, but the risk increases as the sea level rises. Six hundred oil drilling platforms lie in the Gulf of Mexico within forty miles of the coast. Services for these platforms reach Port LaFourche by way of Louisiana's highway 1, much of which lies no more than 4 feet above sea level. The storm surge of a moderate hurricane could easily destroy a section of that highway and reduce U. S. oil producing capability by twenty percent until repairs could be made. Should a hurricane hit New Orleans with 110 mph winds, civil defense authorities predict that water would stand 13 feet deep in the old city and 25,000 to 100,000 people would lose their lives. Every inch of rise in sea level, increases the risk of such a catastrophe.

Far away in North Dakota, the people have just experienced the warmest decade in history. Because warm weather draws moisture into the clouds from which it falls as rain, the area enjoyed long growing seasons and plenty of rain. Farmers harvested bumper crops. By 2002, the warm spell was over, but farmers counting on the weather they had been enjoying, started planting early crops. Heavy snow and frost in May killed sprouting corn before it emerged from the soil. A second planting succumbed to extreme drought. Torrential rains came eventually, but too late to save the crops.

Climate scientists have warned that erratic weather–hot, cold, wet, dry–is an early effect of global warming. Floods, droughts, and storms are expected to increase in frequency and severity as global warming proceeds. To farmers in North Dakota, it looks like they already have.

Global warming is aptly named for the good reason that its effects are widespread. The transfer of atmospheric and oceanic heat modifies climate at different latitudes. If heat were evenly distributed all over the earth, we would expect the climate to be much the same at any given latitude all the way round the earth. But heat isn't evenly distributed and variations in its distribution are significant. For example, Spain, which lies at the same latitude as New York, has a climate more like Florida, which lies some ten degrees of latitude south of New York.

Heat spreads by convection from equatorial regions toward polar regions. Temperature changes from global warming are small near the equator, but they increase with latitude and reach a maximum in polar regions. Consequently, the Intergovernmental Panel on Climate Change (IPCC) predicted that the extent of global warming for the 21st century would average from 2.7° C (5° F) at the equator to 11°C (20°F) at the poles.

When increasing temperatures cause the melting of polar snow, the melting adds pure water to the ocean. Pure water dilutes the ocean's salinity and thereby causes shifts in ocean currents. The Gulf Stream now warms northern Europe, but if it were to shift to a more southerly location, northern Europe might become as cold as the Hudson Bay area, which occupies the same latitudes as northern Europe.

If these facts about climate change leave you with a "ho-hum" feeling, perhaps the threat of tropical and semi-tropical diseases spreading to areas farther from the equator will capture your attention. Many of these diseases–malaria, dengue fever, yellow fever, several kinds of encephalitis–are mosquito-borne. According to the Centers for Disease Control, the United States already sees 1200 cases of malaria per year and 100 to 200 cases of dengue fever. In the 1990s, the hottest decade on record, outbreaks of malaria were seen in Texas, Florida, Georgia, Michigan, and New Jersey. Some occurred as far north as Toronto. Most cases are thought to have arisen from parasites picked up by travelers to countries where malaria is endemic. However, the United States has a vast population of *Anopheles* mosquitoes capable of carrying malaria parasites. Should a few patients be bitten by the mosquitoes, the disease could become endemic. The emerging disease of this century is caused by West Nile virus, which affected 3400 Americans in the first 10 months of 2001 and caused 188 deaths.

Hantavirus pulmonary syndrome, a generally lethal lung infection, emerged in southwestern U. S. in 1993. Ordinarily carried by rodents, this disease can jump from one human to another when people inhale virus particles.

I suppose you have just learned more than you wanted to know about global warming. However, you need to understand the danger to American citizens from climate change, especially its deleterious effects on agriculture and the increased risk of serious infectious diseases. Our leaders have refused to sign the Kyoto Protocol, which was designed to limit the use of fossil fuels and with it, the accumulation of greenhouse gases responsible for global warming.

The time has come for America to do its share to stabilize global climate by greatly reducing our dependence on oil. We can phase out oil and phase in solar and wind energy as these energy sources become economically feasible. I think concerned citizens will need to take the lead in this venture because our government seems not to have the will to do it. We can start by making a commitment to walk, cycle, car pool, or use public transportation wherever and however we can. We can also conserve on heating and air conditioning and boycott businesses and industries that fail to use clean energy to meet their needs. Finally, we can support non-governmental organizations (NGOs) and help them grow powerful enough to pressure our government to stop global warming.

I hope that global public opinion will force our president to sign the Kyoto Protocol and our Congress to legislate reductions in atmospheric carbon dioxide. If, like Icarus, our politicians still ride high on feathers and wax, we will be compelled to organize a grass roots movement to vote them out of office. We can do that if we convince the sixty percent of our citizens who don't ordinary vote that their votes can make a difference. We can elect people who will deal effectively with global warming–tax fossil fuels, subsidize wind, solar, and other forms of clean energy, establish efficient rapid transit systems, and expand the Centers for Disease Control to deal with tropical diseases as they appear in our warmer environment. If every eligible voter realizes that clean renewable energy is the most promising and most profitable technology that any economy can have, we can cure ourselves of the Icarus Syndrome.

Seasons

Lots of people love summer and hate winter, but I'm part of a smaller group that hates summer and really enjoys autumn and winter. Maybe it's a good thing people have no control over the seasons because we would never agree on what season we should be having.

Here in the "ridge and valley" section of Pennsylvania where my husband and I came for a slower-paced retirement, autumn is a glorious time of year. I celebrate its arrival because it means I can look forward to a whole cycle of enjoyable seasons before I need face another summer.

Autumn sharpens my senses. After an oppressive, sticky summer, the first hint of autumn makes me come alive. I inhale cool, crisp morning air and watch as timid sunlight disperses the morning mist. I sniff again at the fresh, clean air. Frost sends some people indoors until spring, but it invigorates and renews me. I'm ready to do things.

I think of autumn as the start of a new year, probably because of the many years I spent in school, first as a student, then as a teacher. No matter that I'm retired, neither a student nor a teacher these days, when autumn arrives I still put away the slovenly stuff of summer and clear the cobwebs out of my brain. I start new projects or make fresh starts on those that have been languishing over the summer.

School buses rattling through my neighborhood are music to my ears. I choke up on my own nostalgia when I see youngsters, clad in new jeans and sports shoes, standing at bus stops swinging shiny lunch boxes and toting stiff backpacks. Those packs filled with unfamiliar books remind me of how excited I used to get about new textbooks. When I talk with neighborhood kids, I find they have different opinions about the start of a new school year.

"Yeah, I like the challenge," says one young lass.

"The new books are neat," says a fellow as he shows me his science book.

One just shrugs, "Ho, hum. Another year."

Regardless of their attitudes about school, all the youngsters seem to burst forth from the afternoon bus with renewed energy. They run home, toss down their backpacks, and grab a snack. Soon a cadre of neighborhood kids collects in the middle of an otherwise quiet residential street. They dodge occasional cars until they have savored every last minute of precious daylight.

Compared to more northerly locations, day lengths change fairly slowly here. Autumn lingers as late-blooming hostas drop their blossoms and Concord grapes mature to plump, purple orbs. When I hear that a hard freeze is predicted, I hurry to harvest the last tomatoes and green peppers in my backyard garden. I savor little snatches of Indian summer, mostly because I know it won't get too hot or last too long.

"John, let's go sit on the deck and enjoy the late afternoon sun on the white birch tree."

"Good idea. We won't be able to do it much longer this year."

Soon our trees will discard their withering, superfluous leaves and prepare for winter, but not before they sally forth with one of nature's most spectacular displays. Right in our own backyard we enjoy golden birch leaves, maroon-colored dogwood foliage, bright red berries on a mountain ash, and variegated leaves on a towering maple.

Once the leaves are down, we rake them into a thick layer over the vegetable garden, thinking our labors are a small price to pay for the pleasures of our trees and vegetable garden. We think of almost-fresh produce in our freezer as we clear away asparagus fronds and scatter straw over dormant strawberry plants. We declare yet another year's garden worth every drop of sweat, and look forward to a winter respite, and a new batch of seed catalogs.

Chilly days let us indulge one of life's most exquisite luxuries–pulling on a favorite sweater for the first time of the season. To find my old white cardigan, I rummaged through clothes that seemed old and tired when I tucked them away last spring. Now I'm surprised at how inviting they look. Even a shabby sweatshirt I had planned to recycle gets a new lease on life. It's just right for raking up the last of the leaves. My stocking cap and woolly mittens feel so much better than the sweaty skin I remember from summer. Dressed for the weather, I enjoy the rustle of leaves as I walk in the cool woods again. I feel sorry for people who live in the tropics and will never know the pleasure of a warm sweater on a chilly day.

Toward the end of autumn, I begin to think about Thanksgiving and celebrating the harvest. Even though I don't depend on my harvest for a bountiful meal, my interest in gardening helps me honor the holiday's original meaning. Our clan gathers all at once or in tandem for a feast. Petty football rivalries pale as we renew family bonds and the time for goodbyes comes too soon. Leftovers, smouldering embers in a fireplace, and good feelings mark the culmination of Thanksgiving, and with it, the best of the autumn season.

Soon winter arrives, and things that make autumn enjoyable get even better. If putting on a sweater in autumn is nice, snuggling into a hooded parka on the first really cold day is pure delight. A crisp winter day puts a spring in my step and joy in my heart. By the winter solstice, I've watched the temperature drop and heard the wind whistle around our house. After a few weeks I start to like winter better from inside the house. My body wants to hibernate–cancel night meetings and spend long evenings indoors curled up with a good book.

I like to look out at the bare, black tree limbs silhouetted against a somber, buttermilk sky. When that sky changes to a pearly-white blanket, I know it will snow. Every year I still get excited when I see the first snowflakes. Just when I'm sick to death of brown grass and decaying leaves, I wake up to a dusting of snow. Even if it melts by noon, it's a harbinger of better times. Soon a real snow covers the drab world in white and casts a spell of silence on my town. Cars and buses glide noiselessly on snow-packed streets and transform my manic world into a peaceful place, at least for a glorious day or two.

When the snow gets deep enough to crunch under my feet, I grab a ski pole for balance and go walking in fresh snow, my senses on high alert. Darkness comes early and lights twinkle in the distance. Icy, wind-buffeted flakes sting my face. I stick my tongue out to taste this year's snow, knowing it will taste the same as it did last year and every year before that. Wood smoke floating from chimneys tells of crackling fires on cozy hearths. I saunter along until my tingling toes send me home to stomp my boots, brush my coat, and go inside.

By morning my town has an honest-to-goodness Currier and Ives look, and I begin to dare hope we will have a white Christmas. That always casts a kindlier spirit on the annual siege of mercantile mania. Our biggest snows arrive in January. That's when we make sure we have enough food on hand and I start to have happy thoughts of being snowbound. I make myself comfy, gather things to read and write, and enjoy the peace and quiet. Soon my peace is shattered by reports that heavy snow and strong winds have snapped power lines and left many people without heat. Our natural gas, convection stove will warm us and our food without electricity, but people who are dependent on electricity can't enjoy being snowbound. Within days, workers restore power and clear the streets. Life resumes its frantic pace.

Winters are enjoyable when one has a warm home, but they would be most unpleasant spent in a cave, a lean-to in the forest, or a sod house on a windy prairie. I wouldn't like huddling around a fireplace in a log cabin, turning to warm first one side and then the other side of my body like meat on a spit. Experiencing winter for yet another year sets me to pondering why countries in cold climates, especially the Scandinavian countries, are among the world's most advanced and civilized societies. They offer the best living conditions to be found anywhere on earth. These nearly classless societies have very little poverty and they offer housing, health care, and education to all their citizens. Does a cold climate challenge people to invent ways to survive and enjoy winter? Does it make people want to be sure that no one goes without the necessities of life? Does it stimulate ambition? Does it foster compassion? I wonder.

After a few snowfalls here in Pennsylvania, winter begins to lose its grip. The sun's rays get stronger and the days lengthen. My favorite season ebbs away to its own bad end. Great mounds of snow plowed to the edges of parking lots disintegrate into rivulets. Snow along roadways turns to dirty slush. Snow in my back yard melts away, exposing decaying leaves and the thick layer of mud in my garden. All I can do then is to gather up my seed catalogs and plan for spring.

Many of my friends are downright ecstatic over the first crocuses, daffodils, and other signs of spring, and they are flamboyant in their equinox celebrations. I can celebrate the equinox as a symbol of new births, new growth, new beginnings. But when spring arrives, summer's not far behind and I can't bring myself to celebrate the imminence of heat, humidity, and mosquito bites.

To give spring its due, it does alleviate cabin fever and encourage people to get outside and greet their neighbors.

Hi, Bob," I say for the first time since fall. "Did you enjoy your trip to Georgia?"

"Oh, yes. Did you have a good winter?"

"Sure did. Flew to Yellowknife in Canada's Northwest Territories where we saw some spectacular Northern Lights." We chat a while before I go back into the house.

In a few days I come out to start preparing the garden for spring planting and I find MUD. Mud disables my shovel and clogs the tines of my tiller. It clings so thick to my shoe soles that I walk like an old-fashioned deep sea diver with lead-weighted boots. Sticky, repulsive spring mud sets me longing for the pristine whiteness of fresh snow.

Spring also ushers in lawn tending and housecleaning. Weed killers and fertilizers produce luxuriant overgrowth. They only makes the grass grow faster and need mowing more often. I use only enough of these insults to the earth to keep from being ostracized by my neighbors. Mowing days get progressively warmer. Dreadful, hot, sticky, humid summer is just around the corner. I try to do my spring housecleaning before summer arrives.

Spring cleaning is easier now than in the days of my childhood when soot from a coal furnace and dust from gravel roads permeated the entire house. Every spring we washed curtains, bedspreads, and blankets, and turned and vacuumed mattresses. We washed windows and woodwork and captured cobwebs from twelve-foot ceilings. Any carpet we could carry, we took out and hung on the clothes line and beat the dust out of it. If I take this half-century long view, I can find joy in my smaller burden of spring housecleaning.

On pleasant days when I have no urgent garden chores, I join my husband on a short walk.

"Oh, look, John. Somebody has cut down that great giant maple tree."

"Well, I see the stump. But I don't remember what kind of tree was there. Maybe there was something wrong with the tree."

"Could be. I suppose we'll never know, but I'm sorry we've lost a big tree."

Then John asks, "What's that I hear?"

"The only thing I hear is a bird singing."

"I think that's the first time I've heard a bird sing in years. This new hearing aid must really be better than the old one."

"Yes, it is better and I think that's great."

I don't have much time for walks in late May and early June because I'm busy tilling soil and planting vegetables. Then, all of a sudden, school's out and strawberries and humidity are in.

Summertime "when the livin' is easy?" Not for me. Gnats get in my eyes and ears. Mosquitoes love me–to eat, that is. They leave itchy welts the size of silver dollars, and now that West Nile virus has been found in the area, they might transmit that disease. Stinging insects infuse me with venom that sends me to the emergency room, and that ruins my day. As if the bugs can't make enough trouble, plants attack me, too. Green bean and corn plants make me itch. Poison ivy causes weepy blisters on my skin and makes me look like something out of a horror movie until cortisone makes me look human again. Even the sun isn't my friend. I don't sunburn easily, but when my skin gets hot it develops itchy red splotches. Sun screen doesn't help, so I just try not to go out in the sun.

Somehow I muddle through summer. The thing that makes me bear up is anticipating my best yet garden yield for the year. I have set new records the last five years. This past summer was not a record, but having some goodies in the freezer at season's end is sufficient reward to get me back in the garden every summer.

Summer doesn't bother me when I'm inside our air-conditioned house. I write. I read. I catch up on mending. We entertain summer guests by taking them to get ice cream cones at the university creamery. That's a treat we allow ourselves only when we have company.

I hate to admit that I need air conditioning when my friends are enjoying summer's easy livin'. I like to think I'm an environmentalist, but resorting to air-conditioning fails to contribute to that image. In winter I wear a sweater and keep the thermostat down. Come oppressive summer days, my environmentalism evaporates faster than the sweat on my brow. I crank up the air conditioner, suffer self-inflicted guilt, and count the days 'til autumn.

Garden Fever

Every spring my head has an attack of "garden fever." And every spring it's harder to convince my body to cope with another garden season. Arthritic aches make gardening less of a pleasure than it once was, but any gardening I can manage helps to keep me living closer to the earth. It still allows me to leave a smaller footprint on my environment than if I planted grass instead of food plants and bought produce delivered by truck from hundreds of miles away.

During the first warm days of March I spread dried manure on the asparagus bed, hoping spring rains will wash the nutrients down to the roots. I also toss a little on the places where I'll soon see tender shoots of rhubarb. I give the hollies, rhododendrons, and azaleas their semi-annual fix of acid-rich fertilizer. I know commercial fertilizer is a "no-no" among organic gardeners. I'm sorry I haven't the energy to comply. I make as much compost as I can, work it into my soil, and supplement it with a bare minimum of "bag" fertilizer.

On another warm day, I prune the grape vines. Every year I think I'll master that art, that I'll really cut away last year's thickest canes and all but a few of the new canes. So far I haven't managed. My vines still have too many leafy canes and only a small crop of puny grapes.

In late April I rake excess straw off the strawberry bed. Every time I do this, I wonder if the long-standing practice of straw mulching is the reason these luscious fruits are called strawberries. When the strawberry plants start blooming in May, I fertilize them to encourage berry production.

The rewards of spring gardening and perennials begin in early May, unless, of course, it's one of those years when outdoor temperature and rainfall are particularly fickle. Sometimes we cut tender asparagus stalks for dinner every other night for a month or more. This year we had frost two weeks later than usual and the asparagus tips were frostbitten. We can make stewed rhubarb any time we want it all summer provided we cut it regularly. We start picking luscious strawberries in mid-June. My new ever-bearing strawberries should start to produce this spring. They're not really ever-bearing, but they do produce a second crop of berries. Maybe this year I'll find out when that happens.

Although perennials bring forth their bounty every spring with little special work, annual vegetables need some work to get them started. Once they get established, they provide a continuous supply of vegetables until frost and sometimes even later. I start by tilling any remains of last fall's leaves into the soil to add nutrients and organic material. One of the trickiest parts of "making garden," is finding a day when the soil has just the right moisture content. If it's cold and soggy, it sticks to the tiller. If it's hard and dry, it makes a dust storm. When soil moisture is just right, I enjoy watching the soil crumble and roll before the tiller and smell its earthy aroma.

I plant peas as early as I can prepare the soil. In fact, one of my friends advises that peas should be in by St. Patrick's Day. I almost made it one year only to have the seeds rot in the ground. Here in Pennsylvania, mid-April is a better bet for the first planting and early May for the second. Along with peas I plant lettuce and spinach and set out broccoli plants. As soon as seeds sprout, I have trouble with garden pests. Groundhogs like broccoli as much as I do, and the rabbits adore lettuce. Last year I threw nylon garden netting over these crops and kept the varmints out. I hope it works again this year.

Come May, I begin tilling in earnest. My small tiller readies more soil for planting in an hour than I can prepare in a whole day with a shovel and hoe. With the threat of frost over by mid May, I can plant the first rows of green beans and corn, and follow them with second and third plantings at two-week intervals. By late May the soil is usually warm enough to set out tomato, green pepper, and basil plants and to sow seeds for cucumbers, yellow squash, and zucchini. When the zucchini is in, the garden is in. I sit back and relax on the deck and watch it grow.

Well, not quite. The trouble with relaxing to watch a garden grow is that weeds grow faster than the edible plants. Among gardening tasks, weeding takes the most self-discipline. It's tedious, boring work that needs doing over and over again, and it promises only the delayed gratification of eating the vegetables eventually. If I succeed in helping the edible plants beat out the weeds, I soon start to reap my reward in the form of a nearly daily basket of fresh vegetables–lettuce, spinach, and peas through June and into July and green beans, green peppers, and zucchini in July and August, and tomatoes and corn in August and September. Many vegetables continue to produce into September if I pick them regularly and keep the plants watered.

When our local weather report warns of frost, usually during the first half of October, I hurry out to pick the last of the tomatoes and green peppers because they are most often damaged by frost. There endeth another gardening season, except for broccoli and leafy vegetables that continue to grow. Starting in March and gardening into October is quite a long enough season for me. By then the freezer is full of goodies, and I'm ready for a rest from the garden, except for the possibility of harvesting fresh broccoli on Christmas day.

Our Monax Moments

We've had, not Kodak Moments, but Monax Moments in our back yard, times when a groundhog with the Latin name *Marmata monax* leisurely clambered from under our shed to sample garden treats. Monax lives in a slower lane, too. We think Monax is a male because he's been with us for two summers and hasn't yet emerged with a trail of little Monaxies.

From Monax's point of view, the area under our shed is a perfect home. It offers space for a maze of burrows in a protected, sheltered area. It's warm in winter, cool in summer, and always out of reach of my hoe. Furthermore, my garden and five others in neighboring yards all offer tempting delectables.

During his first summer, Monax made several appearances, each time devouring newly matured green beans or leaving half-eaten tomatoes. We'd be happier without our Monax Moments. They just don't fit with our laid-back, low-stress retirement living. Monax is a nuisance, plain and simple. But he's here and he does present a challenge.

One autumn when spring had been too hot too soon to raise good broccoli, I set out a dozen large, healthy broccoli plants and fitted them with plastic collars to protect against cutworms. They grew nicely and were ready to harvest when I promised myself one evening that I would pick broccoli the next day. Overnight, Monax picked broccoli for himself, leaving only thoroughly trimmed, naked stalks. Another Monax Moment.

I sacrificed several perfectly good tomatoes to bait a Hav-a-Heart trap, but Monax didn't take the bait. I even borrowed a bee-bee gun and lobbed a few volleys in Monax's direction. He lumbered toward the shed and crawled under. His slow, deliberate pace made it clear that my marksmanship didn't scare him.

Winter came and snow blanketed the garden. Monax ensconced himself deep in a burrow beneath the shed. Then one sunny spring morning, he came out. While robins stirred up a fury of dry leaves searching for worms, Monax emerged. I didn't see him yawn, but he stretched himself as luxuriously as a groundhog can. He nibbled a few columbine leaves. Then he spied the spring broccoli and went–well, er–groundhog wild. I threw a rock but it was so wide of the mark that Monax finished eating before he sauntered over to the shed and slid into his hole.

That year we had Monax Moments nearly every morning all summer. Once I got some rodent poison and poked it well back into Monax's hole. Of course, Monax must have thoroughly contaminated his belly fur with arsenic as he crawled through it, but it didn't seem to bother him. Next, I bought a pellet gun and appropriate ammunition. I had so much trouble loading, pumping, and aiming the gun that Monax got bored and left. Later, when I finally managed to lob a shot in his direction, he merely moved a little faster. Next I used the garden hose to flood the area under the shed. I let it run until I was sure the water must be at least a foot deep in the burrows under the shed. Monax gave no sign of distress. He wasn't even wet when he came out to sample tender young green beans.

A few days later I found Monax sitting up on his haunches like a well-trained terrier nibbling strawberries. What audacity! A net kept the birds out of the strawberries, but Monax crawled under it and ate to his heart's content. I had worked hard to grow strawberries and I was furious. I bought a sulfur bomb, stationed a team of family and friends around the shed, some with shovels to cover smoke leaks with dirt and some with hoses to spray water if the shed floor caught fire. A courageous member of my team lit the fuse and put the bomb under the shed. A little smoke leaked for a few minutes. After that, nothing. We'd conquered Monax. Or so we thought. The following morning, we found the telltale claw prints and disturbed earth at the entrance to Monax's burrow just like we had seen all summer.

The next episode began when a lean and hungry young ground hog graced us with his presence. We dubbed him Son-of-a-Monax. He was the spittin' image of Monax-the-Elder, except that the Elder was grossly obese and Sonny hadn't yet had enough to eat to lose his sleek youthful appearance. Sonny didn't damage many vegetables, but he didn't deserve much credit for self-discipline. The fact was that Monax-the-Elder had already done almost all the damage that could be done.

Fall moved into winter and Sonny crawled under the front addition to our house and snuggled into a burrow far away from harsh winds and icy plants. I know he stirred periodically because I sometimes heard him banging around directly under the floor. We saw nothing of either Monax-the-Elder or Sonny on Groundhog's Day. It seemed to me that any self-respecting groundhog ought to at least make an appearance on his holiday, especially here in Pennsylvania, where our town of Punxsutawney is hailed as the capital of groundhog country.

One fine day in March we found Sonny sitting in front of the garage door looking like he was just waiting for us to get home. Yet when we got out of the car, he dashed back under the house. We still hadn't seen Monax-the-Elder, but Sonny had been out and about every warm day helping with our spring yard clean-up. He trimmed the lower branches of several shrubs and cut back the yucca plants. I thought yucca plants were so fibrous nothing would eat them. Well, Sonny would and Sonny did. He gobbled foot-long blades right down to thumb-length stubs. No rabbit could have done that, I said to myself as I surveyed the damage.

Nearly every day I saw that Son-of-a-Monax sitting out by the shed just daring me to plant something. And I was ready to plant peas. That called for a showdown. Whenever I saw him I opened the kitchen window and beat two foil pans together. He scampered away. Every time. Right under the shed. That was in spite of the fact that the previous summer a young neighbor had laid a border of large concrete paving stones all the way around the shed.

"Great job, David," I said when he had hefted the stones into position. "That'll surely keep the groundhogs out from under the shed."

"I hope so," said David. He didn't sound very sure, and I wondered if he knew more about groundhogs than I did.

A week later I was looking out the window and saw Sonny charge out of a large hole three feet from the edge of the shed. He had burrowed under the stone and surfaced well clear of any obstruction.

"That's it. That's the final affront," I mumbled aloud, but Sonny paid no attention. Then I remembered our new phone directory. I read the current entries under pest control. Ah ha, a new listing that promised removal of woods pests. I called immediately. Mr. Benner came the same evening and set three traps around the perimeter of the shed. He baited them with freshly diced, ripe apple. Then he applied a few drops of two different red solutions.

"What's that stuff?" I asked.

"These are lures. One smells like groundhogs, the other has a fruity smell."

The morning after the traps were set I looked out the dinette window every time I passed it. While drinking my midmorning coffee, I saw Sonny sniffing around the trap. I grabbed the binoculars I usually use for bird watching, and watched as Sonny went into the trap. Almost all the way in. I held my breath. Then Sonny backed out and sat on the ground while he ate several pieces of apple the trapper had scattered in front of the cage. He sniffed the front part of the cage again. And backed out again.

"Come on, Sonny! Into the trap," I whispered to myself, even though I wanted to yell. I stood rooted to the floor with binoculars frozen to my face waiting for the next move. He went down the hole into the burrow. After what seemed like an hour but was really only a minute or two, he came back out and sniffed around the cage again.

Finally, Sonny went into the cage--all the way in, over the treadle, and all the way to the back of the cage. The gate crashed down behind him. He paced. He lay down dejectedly. He paced some more. I know it's an anthropomorphic fantasy, but that animal really did seem to have a bewildered expression on his face. He rocked the cage. He tried to dig through the bottom of it. He grabbed the treadle and jumped up and down, shaking the whole cage. He shook the cage so hard the small sheet of plywood the trapper had placed on top of the cage for shade slid off.

That afternoon the trapper came and took that Son-of-a-Monax for his last ride.

"Bye, Sonny," I said as Sonny went bravely to his reward. "I'll send Monax-the-Elder to join you as soon as I can."

From Rural Mailboxes to E-Mail

Times have changed in the years since I held Grandma's hand as we walked down the lane from the farmhouse to the mailbox. Today, we now communicate with each other in less charming but more efficient ways. Our metal, breadloaf-shaped mailbox was tightly anchored to the top of a fence post set in a pull-out next to the highway. Six days a week the mail carrier stopped at our box. It was a great day, indeed, when I got tall enough to open and close the mailbox and was allowed to go get the mail by myself. I felt very grown-up even though I still couldn't read a word of the mail I carried to the house.

I didn't expect any of the mail to be mine. After I started learning to read, I realized that I could now expect there might be something exciting in the mailbox for me—a new *Jack and Jill or Wee Wisdom* magazine or a letter from my cousin, Royce. Royce entered school a year before I did and could read much better than I. He liked to use big words I didn't yet know.

By the time I really was grown up, I had learned that mail came in the form of bills as well as letters from friends and relatives. I also knew that it could bring bad news as well as good. Now that most of my news comes by e-mail or telephone, what the postal service delivers is limited to magazines, an occasional package, yuletide greeting cards, and a lot of junk mail that goes directly to the recycling bag without ever being opened.

E-mail has superceded postal deliveries for timely messages so much that we call what the carrier brings "snail mail." Sometimes I get a dozen or more e-mail messages a day and only a small number of them are jokes. I get messages from my brother, two sons, one granddaughter, and quite a few friends. Since none of them are, or ever were, great letter writers, I'm thankful for e-mail because I hear from them much more often.

E-mail is the greatest advance in communication since the Pony Express. It arrives quietly and waits patiently in a convenient location to be read. I don't need to go out in the rain to collect it. E-mail allows efficient communication with the outside world without disrupting my day or setting my teeth on edge with strident, insistent ringing like the telephone does. I can answer at my convenience and not when it screams at me.

E-mail is better than the old multi-party phone line my family had when I was a child. I can send the same message to many people, just like always happened willy-nilly on the party line. But with e-mail, I, and not the phone company, decide who those people are. They can be across the back fence, across town, or across the ocean. All receive the same message.

Not long ago, I used e-mail to plan a trip to Eastern Europe. At one point I got weary of making arrangements and shuddered to think how much on-the-spot negotiation remained to be done in countries I had never before visited and where I knew nothing of the language. I quit and went to bed. The next morning I had an e-mail from a travel agent in Sofia, Bulgaria offering to meet my husband and me at the airport, arrange a hotel in our price range, and deliver us to it for a modest fee. I responded immediately to accept the offer.

Some people find e-mail an impersonal, unfriendly way to communicate. Well, if they knew what a procrastinator I am when I must write letters, address envelopes, and find stamps, they would be forced to conclude that e-mail is better than no mail. If they knew how an irritating phone call disrupts my thoughts or ruins a perfect sentence in its birthing, they might see that although e-mail can be impersonal, at least it's not aggravating and intrusive. Answering is similarly quick and non-intrusive.

Unfortunately, e-mail can be as offensive a purveyor of junk as snail-mail, actually worse, if you count the possibility of receiving pornographic messages. At least e-mail ads don't waste paper or cause a delivery service to expend fossil fuel and wear out automotive parts just to distribute them to mailboxes. And, I don't need to bag or bundle e-mail for recycling.

The really troubling thing about e-mail is that it might contain a computer "virus." Carelessly opening an "infected" message can unleash a virus to cannibalize or scramble programs and files. If we open only e-mails from known senders and quickly delete unidentified flying e-mails, we reduce the virus threat. I guess anti-virus software works, but from what I've read it also spurs on the "one-upmanship" between virus creators and the people who write virus-detecting software. In the long run, it probably speeds up the evolution of both the viruses and the software to combat them.

The problem with computer viruses resembles the competition between pathogenic bacteria and antibiotics in the natural world. This battle has raged since antibiotics first came into use eighty years ago. In fact, microbes and natural antimicrobial substances have been competing in nature for millions of years, long before we humans knew anything about their clandestine activities. Each new antibiotic packs a more powerful wallop against certain bacteria. Almost as soon as a new antibiotic comes into use, some bacteria become resistant to it. Because antibiotic resistance involves a genetic change, the progeny of resistant bacteria are also antibiotic resistant. As susceptible bacteria die, only resistant organisms survive and reproduce. And so it goes with each new antibiotic sowing the seeds of its own ineffectiveness.

I've not encountered a computer virus on my own computer, and most of my e-mail is friendly and useful. I don't waste much time with busy signals on the phone or waiting for an answer to reach me by snail-mail. If I really want to know how someone feels about something, I call that person on the phone and hope I don't get a busy signal. The tone and inflection of a voice tells me things that written messages can never do regardless of whether they arrive by e-mail or snail mail. But for written communications, I'm sold on e-mail. It works for me.

In spite of the shortcomings of snail mail, I don't want to part with the mailbox at the end of our drive. It's the same kind of breadloaf-shaped mailbox that Grandma had when I was a little girl. And sometimes I find something exciting in it.

Spirit of Blue Knob

At 3034 feet elevation, Blue Knob is a mountain, at least by Pennsylvania standards. To me, it's more than a mountain. It's a perfect place to enjoy all the benefits of life in a slower lane. It's where I can feel the steady procession of seasonal changes and the capriciousness of weather. It's a place to observe the sun and moon and to ponder the mysteries of the stars, a humbling place that makes me glad to be a small part of this infinite universe.

Winter stays so long at Blue Knob that it shortens the frost-free growing season and crowds the other seasons. Spring comes late, summer is contracted, and autumn finishes early.

When spring arrives, the blossoms of yellow colt's foot line the road to the ski slopes. Their squatty stems barely poke above the rocky soil. Birds just back from their winter homes declare their territories in song with every sunrise. Trees leaf out as if to sieve the sun's rays onto the forest floor. Native rhododendrons and mountain laurels insert themselves along the edges of the forest and wherever they find semi-sunny spaces. By late spring, they grace the mountain with their pale pink or white blossoms.

Summer brings heat and humidity but mainly at mid-day on the mountain, while the valley swelters day and night. Sunshine makes water droplets on the grass sparkle like diamonds. It also brings out the wildflowers. Pearly Everlasting spreads its button-like blossoms over highland meadows and Queen Anne's lace towers over the red clover and crown vetch that cover the ground near the trails. Fern fronds make a fluffy green blanket on the forest floor. Screeching tree frogs shatter the peace of summer evenings. I know summer is past its peak when a scummy green algal bloom lays across the surfaces of ponds.

Autumn brings the first frost and the withering of fern fronds to ragged bronze flags. Maple and oak leaves paint the forest in earthy tones of gold and orange, red and brown that stand out against towering evergreens. This is my favorite time of year for walking in the woods.

Soon enough, blustery winds usher in winter and snow dresses the brown earth in white. In years past, I pulled grandchildren on sleds or helped build snow people. Alas, times have changed. My arthritic joints and botched hip replacement caution me against ice under foot. The grandchildren have traded sledding and making snow-people for skiing and more exciting adventures. I stay inside by the crackling fire and look out at the pristine snow. These days, that's winter joy enough for me.

The features of any season are enhanced by the contemplation of the inexorable cycle of seasons flowing from one to the next, year after year like variations on a symphonic theme. More important than the delights of any season is the reassuring knowledge that the seasons will progress dependably, even relentlessly–autumn to winter to spring to summer, to autumn again.

At Blue Knob the weather is as capricious as the seasons are steadfast. Sudden changes in the weather make me tingle with excitement when I'm on the mountain. A spring day can begin shrouded in fog and clear to bright sunshine by noon. Then it can sally forth with thunder, lightning, and a torrential downpour in the afternoon, only to close with a glorious sunset.

Fog is a frequent companion on the mountain. It steals in and spreads its blanket without warning. It casts an eerie silence, a surrealistic mood that masks the ordinary and mixes fantasy with reality. If fog hangs below the summit, it leaves the mountaintop in bright sunshine and the valley in dark shadow.

Fall rains come more as drizzle than down pour. Strong winds whip the drizzle into frozen missiles that sting the skin and coat the ground with shimmering ice. From inside looking out, the ice has an awesome beauty. On foot, it is treacherous, even for people with good, young legs. Snow comes in fluffy flakes that float gently to the ground or as icy bullets on diagonal paths at the whim of gravity-thwarting winds. Ultimately, snow makes great white mounds in some places and frail coatings that barely hide the dead brown terrain in others.

Blue Knob provides a vantage point for observing the movements of the sun and moon. In winter I enjoy watching the sun rise above the horizon without getting up early and drop below it well before bedtime. Plentiful clouds make sunrises and sunsets particularly enchanting here on the mountain. I"m fascinated by the way the elevation seems to magnify seasonal changes in the sun's angle with the horizon. In summer, the sun appears to rise in the northeast, traverses a wide arc high in the sky, and sets in the northwest. In winter, it goes through these motions in a much tighter arc closer to the southern horizon. When the sky is clear at night on top of the mountain, the moon looks closer than at sea level, much closer than can be accounted for by elevation. Sometimes it looks like I could just reach out and touch it.

Star gazing at Blue Knob is spectacular. The mountaintop is far from city lights and manufactured obstructions. Stars come out faster than I can count them–one, ten, a hundred, an infinite number. They spread themselves far and wide and overwhelm this small, insignificant observer, this nonessential, random blip on the vast radar screen of an awesome universe.

Blue Knob enriches my slow-paced life with joys of my favorite seasons. It assures me of the orderly procession of changes in temperature and moisture that define the seasons. It also guarantees the capriciousness of the weather and the constancy of the sun, moon, and stars. All these attractions define the spirit of Blue Knob, and I'm thankful for it.

On Solstice Trees

Now that my children are grown and my holiday season is less frantic, I have time to enjoy the tree that stands in my living room during the darkest weeks of the year. It's my Solstice Tree. Symbolically, it keeps vigil for the longest night and stands ready to celebrate the return of light. It commemorates human longings for light and hope that predate all major religions. Having a solstice tree allows me to enjoy what it symbolizes without being concerned with troubling religious dogmas.

According to tradition, the sun reaches its lowest point on the horizon, sends its weakest rays, and stays out of view for the longest time at the winter solstice. That's not strictly true. Here in State College, for example, the earliest sunset occurs at about 4:40 PM in early December and the latest sunrise occurs at about 7:38 AM in early January. The duration of daylight stays approximately the same for nearly a month while both the sunrise and the sunset are delayed in a parallel fashion by a total of about ten minutes–sunset from 4:40 to 4:50 and sunrise from 7:28 to 7:38. Fortunately, we needn't fear that our sun will disappear as ancient peoples did when they invented rituals to preserve the sun.

Many of our winter traditions are based on such ancient practices. The Romans celebrated Saturnalia with good-luck gifts, made elaborate costumes to wear in parades, and engaged in riotous merry-making. Scandinavians drank mead around a great yule log, which they believed made the sun shine more brightly. They also worshiped the sacred oak tree and the parasitic mistletoe that hung from its branches. At least a thousand years ago, pagans living in the region that is now Germany worshiped the oak tree. St. Boniface is said to have caught them performing their ceremonies and cut their tree down in anger. When another tree sprang from the roots, St. Boniface took this as a sign of faith.

Trees were first brought indoors in the 16th century. By the 19th century Germans regularly brought trees inside at Christmas time and decorated them with hand-blown glass ornaments. Once while Queen Victoria was visiting in Coburg, Germany, she met Prince Albert. After they were married Prince Albert initiated the custom of indoor decorated trees in London. Britains loved the royal couple and copied their actions, so having decorated, indoor Christmas trees became a tradition. Both my husband's and my families honored that tradition, and we have done so for fifty years. I like calling it a solstice tree because that name is more historically accurate and more closely reflects my beliefs.

Every year as I drag a tattered box that holds our artificial "tinkertoy" tree up from the basement, I think of all the choices we have about indoor trees: real or artificial, live or chopped down, appropriated or purchased.

The first tree I remember was appropriated. One December day in the late1930s when I was about five years old, Mom said, "Let's go get a Christmas tree."

"Good, good," I said as I grabbed my coat and boots.

We bundled ourselves against a sharp west wind. Mom picked up her hatchet, and we climbed into her modest black Chevy. She drove along back roads looking for a wild, unfenced patch of evergreens. When she found a good spot, she pulled off the road and stopped. Hatchet in hand, Mom trudged across the land with me at her heels. The wind made our eyes water so we could hardly see the shapes of trees. We passed a towering oak and saw several stately sycamores down by the creek before we came to a patch of small, scrubby evergreens. We stopped, turned our backs to the wind, and wiped our eyes. Presently, Mom spotted a tree she liked.

"There's a good one," she said as she pointed.

"Get a bigger one, Mom," I urged.

"That one is big enough. We don't want a bigger one."

I cast my eyes downward and dragged the toe of my boot over the cold, bare earth. "I want a bigger one," I said with a stubborn scowl on my face. Mom never took much notice of such faces. She eyed the tree carefully to be sure it was right and then set to work chopping it down.

"What if someone sees you cutting down a tree?" I asked.

"They won't," Mom answered. "Not now. It's already down."

With a whoosh and a thump, the tree hit the ground. We dragged it to the car. Mom hoisted the tree into the trunk and closed the lid gently on the three feet of tree hanging over the bumper. Mom was right, as usual. The tree was big enough. When we got home we dragged it onto the back porch at Grandma's house and stood it in a corner in a bucket of water.

"Let's put it in the parlor," I said.

"No," Mom answered. "Christmas is two weeks away. It will lose needles and it might catch fire in the warm house."

I was disappointed to have to wait such a long time to see that tree in the parlor.

A few days before Christmas, Grandpa nailed boards to the bottom of the tree to make a stand and set the tree in a corner of the parlor, where it stood taller than any of the people. In those days, nobody had metal or plastic stands that could hold water for a tree. Mom got out the lights, fragile glass ornaments, yards of tinsel rope, and leftover tinfoil icicles. We were ready to decorate the tree. We once had a strand of lights with bulbs in the shapes of nursery rhyme characters. Most of those bulbs have burned out, but the Little Bo Peep bulb still lights up. We've replaced the others with ordinary tree light bulbs. As soon as Mom made sure every bulb lit, she put the strands on the tree. Next she arranged swags of tinsel rope. She let me decorate the lower branches with ornaments while she decorated the higher ones. Finally, Mom started draping each tinfoil icicle carefully over the end of a branch.

"I want to hang icicles," I said.

"No," Mom answered. "Not until you can hang them one at a time."

"I can do that now, I promise. Give me a chance."

Mom gave me a few icicles and I carefully pulled them apart and laid them one at a time on the branches. Soon the tree was fully decorated.

Each year when we took down the tree, Mom saved the icicles. Tinfoil was expensive. When World War II demanded all the country's metal resources and none could be squandered on frivolous things, I was really glad Mom had saved the old icicles.

During World War II, more people moved to our area and unfenced property became scarce. Never again would Mom chop down another tree. The Lion's Club and the Boy Scouts started selling trees from tree farms. I think Mom was relieved to be able to buy a tree so conveniently.

After the war when aluminum foil icicles became cheap and plentiful, we replaced our bedraggled, tarnished tin ones. We also bought a metal tree stand and kept it filled with water. Now we could keep a tree up much longer, and I liked that. For several years Mom supervised my tree decorating, but by the time I was twelve, I was chief tree decorator. I kept the job until I got married and moved to Texas.

For the eight years we lived in Texas, we never had what I call a real Christmas—one with children bundled-up and stomping their feet against the chill and the sound of far away bells floating in the cold, crisp air. People reminded me that Christmas originated in a hot, sandy desert, but to me, it isn't Christmas unless it's cold. Regardless of the temperature, we took occasional drives into the countryside where we sometimes saw patches of untended evergreens. We were never tempted to help ourselves because almost all fields had signs that read POSTED–NO TRESPASSING. In spite of all the "everything is big in Texas" braggadocio, the untended evergreens were the scrawniest, scraggliest excuses for trees I'd ever seen.

For our first Christmas as husband and wife, we bought a tiny tree, one string of lights, a bundle of decorative rope, a dozen shiny ornaments, and some icicles. Over the years we moved to a bigger apartment, had a baby, bought a house, and had more babies. Soon we had three pre-schoolers wide eyed with excitement on Christmas morning. I went through the motions of keeping Christmas every year, but I just couldn't get used to celebrating it on a hot, sunny day.

The year we moved to Northern Virginia, we were rewarded with a generous and glorious snowfall. I was ecstatic. This would be a real Christmas. The children, now nearing 3, 5, and 7 made bell-shaped ornaments from egg cartons, coated them with bright tempera paints, and sprinkled them with glitter. Those ornaments wore out long ago, but they brightened many holiday seasons.

A few years later, our oldest child collected cast off trees from all around our neighborhood. With our permission, he stashed them on our screened porch. We knew they burned too hot to be used as regular firewood, but we thought they could be used sparingly for kindling to start fires in our fireplace. Then one night we heard a fire engine on our street. The fire was in the chimney of our next-door neighbor's house, the house closest to our tree stash. As we watched the firemen, we saw sparks flying out of the chimney toward our screened porch. They all seemed to go out before they reached the tree stash, but we had some uneasy moments. We made sure no more sparks were flying before we went to bed, and we got rid of the tree stash the next day.

Later that year a friend told us how she added an ornament to her collection each year to symbolize the most important family event of the year. We adopted the custom the next year. To get started, I created ornaments retroactively, one for each year we had been married–a wedding bell, tiny dolls wrapped in flannel for new babies, a small piece of sheet music for the year my husband first sang in an opera chorus, a scroll for my first college degree, a miniature house for the year we bought our real house. Since that time, we have added an ornament every year, sometimes two or three when we couldn't pick only one of many important events.

The year our fourth child learned to walk in November, we unscrewed the rockers from the family cradle and put our last real tree in it to protect it from curious fingers. The next year we got our "tinkertoy" tree. SOME ASSEMBLY REQUIRED, it said on the box. Indeed! The box contained two sections of wooden dowel for the trunk and thirty-three sturdy green bottle brushes.

One formed the tree top, two rows of four made the next branches, and four rows of six made the lower branches. When we finally got it assembled, we had a fireproof tree that didn't drop needles. We could put it up right after Thanksgiving and keep it up indefinitely. By mid-January even the children were tired of it.

Back in the youth of our artificial tree, people began to celebrate Earth Day. Our recyclable tree would have made a good Earth Day symbol had we taken time to set it up. It has survived being assembled, decorated, and disassembled enough times to bring four children and two grandchildren to adulthood and a third grandchild to middle school. It's still going strong.

When we moved to Pennsylvania, we brought our eco-conscious tree with us. I downsized the tree by cutting a foot off one dowel and appropriating some of its largest bottle- brush limbs for outdoor decorations. Every year when I decorate our little tree, we reminisce about our collection of fifty-odd ornaments. We now have three wedding bells, seven dolls for children and grandchildren, and about a dozen scrolls for high school and college graduations. We use a few of our children's most durable ornaments to symbolize years when raising children was the event of the year. In recent years we have collected ornaments from our travels–a ceramic cat from Egypt, a fur-scrap seal from Greenland, and a zany plastic penguin on skis from Antarctica.

That great little tree stands proud as any hero. It has not only protected us from fires, it has also saved nearly forty real trees from the blows of a hatchet. The ornaments on our tree enrich every holiday season with our best memories. As long as I can assemble it, we'll always have a tree. And I'll call it my Solstice Tree.

Woods as Cathedral

The woods are my cathedral. A stop in the woods means more to me than any visit to a lofty stone cathedral. I like to saunter through a quiet wooded area, especially in autumn when the only sound is the rustle of leaves underfoot. Living a slower-paced life lets me take time to stop and sit on a bench. I listen carefully as a gentle breeze moves through trees, an occasional bird sings out, and now and then a cricket chirps. A young deer darts across an open space and back into the woods, its white tail flagging surrender and its brisk retreat thwarting capture. A mature chipmunk scampers over some fallen branches and disappears under a pile of leaves. Being in the woods creates a peaceful interlude that lets me appreciate my oneness with nature.

Oneness with nature is a fragile thing. Too often the pictures in my mind's eye portray destruction instead. Oil spills from freighters, fragmented habitats, invasion of pristine wilderness, drained wetlands destined to make way for development–they all shatter my oneness with nature.

Oneness with nature is worth the struggle to maintain it. Being in the woods helps, and I like the woods and its nature sounds. Maybe my "likings" were born into me on a farm in southern Indiana. Maybe they hatched after I became a biology major. Maybe my nature connection matured with that of many other Americans who celebrated the first Earth Day on April 22, 1970. By that time my days were filled with family and career obligations. My contact with nature was limited to occasional trips to local parks and vacations to more distant ones. I grabbed and savored opportunities just to sit at a picnic table under a tree and unjangle my nerves. Such are the things that sustain me during demanding, stressful times.

The more environmental biology I learned, the more this knowledge intruded on my innocent love of nature. When I look at a majestic tree in full leaf, I hear sounds of chain saws on the march to destroy it for timber. When I look at a clear, rushing stream in the spring, I have a vision of the run-off from chicken factories and hog farms racing toward such streams.

Now that my husband and I have retired to Pennsylvania, I'm renewing my connections with nature. I'm rediscovering what I have known since my earliest park visiting days: I am happiest, most whole when I'm surrounded by trees. After years of too few woodsy times, I still find that trips to a wooded area soothe my being and remind me that I'm part of an orderly universe. I sense order in nature, the cycles of the seasons with their reassuring sameness. Within these constraints, I applaud the variations that become the spice of life.

When I contemplate the living diversity in the woods, I lament that many species are threatened, then endangered, and finally driven to extinction, sacrificed on the altar of human greed. Every time one species among the rich diversity of life is lost, we humans edge closer to our own extinction.

Having time to sit on a bench in a park or a log in the woods means that I also have time to think about the meaning of life. One question pops up again and again. Are my feelings about nature and the serenity I experience in the woods in any sense religious experiences? If not, I'm bereft of religion. Do woodsy experiences that lift my spirit qualify as spiritual? If not, I have no spiritual experiences. If my experience is neither religious nor spiritual, then I've done without such experiences for seventy years, and I'll probably manage for the rest of my days.

Off and on during the first thirty-some years of my life, I attended services at least sporadically in an assortment of Christian churches. I found them all wanting. No matter how hard I tried, I could not accept a Christian savior or even conceive of a personal god. Specifying a god of a particular gender made matters worse. I held so many beliefs that were outside Christian dogma that I felt like a hypocrite setting foot in a Christian church. I still do.

Judeo-Christian traditions have done much to foster the rape of our environment. The biblical injunction, "Be fruitful and multiply" may have made sense in biblical days when the human population was minuscule. Now with more than six billion people, many of them squandering natural resources and defiling the planet, that injunction is sheer folly. What we need is informed, cautious stewardship of nature in all its magnificent diversity.

If there is a god, it seems to me, it must be some kind of creative and organizing force, something that is part and parcel of the natural universe. I'm much more inclined to try to increase my understanding of that universe than to sit back and blindly worship it. So far, I have found no assurance that there is a god, nor can I be sure there's not. But I keep asking the question. I guess that makes me an inquiring agnostic. I've always been an agnostic, but I didn't muster the courage to say so until I joined a Unitarian Universalist Fellowship. Sometimes I learn things in Sunday services. I like the support and good feeling I get from being part of a group of caring people who share the same concerns and values. But only rarely do I feel a kind of interconnectedness with the rest of creation during a service. When I do feel it, I'm usually looking out the window at a tree-covered ridge in the distance. The closest I come to religious experience still happens in the woods where I'm most likely to feel oneness with nature.

I've rejected the notion of personal salvation in any religious sense in favor of salvation of our planet's ability to sustain life in all its diverse life forms. Today's threats include, but certainly aren't limited to, global warming, depletion of aquifers and other water supplies, pollution of many kinds, destruction of cropland, terrorism, the threat of nuclear war, and the most fundamental of all, overpopulation. To waste effort on a selfish search for personal salvation and the promise of life after death makes no sense to me. It does make sense to focus on reducing the risk of real threats to life on earth, and to try to protect our environment from overpopulation and over-development. When I think about the state of our planet, I want to gnash my teeth and weep for my descendants, who may never know woods as their cathedrals.

There's creativity in the way an embryo develops from one cell into a finished organism–an oyster, a fish, or a human baby. There's creativity and intelligence in the way animals feed and shelter themselves. There's order in all of nature, including in the lives of humans. I've tried equating forces that impose order with god. It sounds good, but it doesn't explain anything. How special forms of orderly molecules aggregate and coalesce to create life is still a mystery. So be it.

Well, I didn't really mean to preach a sermon, but I've done it now and you can take it or leave it. The woods are still my cathedral. Autumn leaves create windows that have all the beauty and elegance of stained glass. Park benches and fallen logs are my pews. Birds form the choir and sing the anthems. No words, no creeds, no robed dignitaries, only a silent, awesome oneness with all creation fills my cathedral. And that's enough.

Football

My husband and I now live in the eleventh of the Big Ten towns. Impossible? Not at all. With football, anything is possible. In this town where we enjoy our retirement years, we have all the cultural benefits of a university, and suffer through its various disruptive forces. For me, football is one of those forces.

I learned nothing about football in my small high school, where we had too few big fellows to make a team. When I went away to college, I didn't understand football (and a lot of other things). I wanted to learn about many things, but football wasn't one of them. I didn't go to football games, even though my student activity pass would have let me in free. I learned a lot in college, but I still didn't learn about football.

One day, quite by chance, I was tutored in football by an Andy Griffith recording. Andy said he ran across some big guys playing with a lopsided ball in a grassy cow pasture surrounded by tiers of seats. He didn't understand what was happening, but he stuck around hoping he could figure it out. The guys seemed to run a short distance and either fall down or get knocked down. An older guy running along the side lines sent some of the guys out of the pasture and held up the action until others came into the fracas. Soon an invigorated pack charged forward.

After consuming enough hot dogs and orange soda to make himself sick, Andy said he had it all figured out. It was a game, and the object of the game was to grab that lopsided ball and "run from one end of that big ol'cow pasture to t'other without gettin' knocked down or steppin' in somethin'."

In the years since Andy explained football, the game has become increasingly popular at both collegiate and professional levels. Billions of dollars change hands every season. Having a winning team is right up there with, or ahead of, the traditional goals of a university–you know, things like intellectual curiosity and academic excellence. I hear lots of talk about football scholarships. Football scholarship? Now that's an oxymoron if I ever heard one.

The football powers at our university have been engaged in one-upmanship with another university over who has the largest stadium. The stadium in my town has undergone "improvement" and now seats more than 100,000 fans. Those with enough money and influence sit in climate-controlled luxury boxes where they can watch the game on television, just like ordinary folks do at home. I doubt that many walk to a window and peer down seventy feet or so to the fifty-yard line and farther to the goal posts. Our stadium might have become the nation's largest except that the current holder of that title got wind of our construction plans and made its own plans. Now both stadiums are larger but the title didn't change hands. I guess our university will just have to make do until the next "ratcheting up" of stadium size.

I am incensed by the outrageous amounts of money that go into construction and other resources for the sake of football. A change in priorities from "football is all" toward human and community needs could have shifted funds from nosebleed bleachers occupied less than a dozen times a year to urgently needed projects in our state. During the last summer of construction, one of the largest cranes in Pennsylvania got a lot of people excited as it hoisted a new scoreboard. The job didn't really require man-on-Mars technology, but it did draw a pastureful of onlookers. In my view, that hoist amounted to the heist of enough money to cover the annual budget of several local social service agencies. We still have hundreds of women without medical care and hundreds of families making it through the month on food stamps, but we have the biggest, newest scoreboard in the Big Ten, at least for now.

The more seats the stadium has, the worse the traffic becomes on football weekends. Transportation planners–people who have never seen a bulldozer or a concrete mixer they didn't love–tell us I-99 will move traffic in and out of our fair city with ease. But that eyesore will only increase traffic in a town already overwhelmed on football weekends by as many as forty thousand extra vehicles, including hundreds of recreational vehicles. The RVs lumber along our streets until they are corralled in three or four cow pastures on the "ag" campus. Traffic backs up for blocks on Friday evenings. Football fans jam all the local restaurants. Tailgate parties, even among those who have no tailgate, keep local citizens awake far into the night.

With more bleachers and more traffic, the construction of more hotels wasn't far behind. Before the finishing touches were on the stadium, at least four national hotel chains had broken ground and staked their claim to some of the spoils of a bigger stadium. We've been invaded, violated, here in our gentle, peaceful town. Of course, we have more soft pillows for the aching heads from the tailgate parties, but we also have a new problem: What other kinds of mega-entertainment will be enticed to invade our town to keep those hotel rooms in use year round?

In addition to the overnighters, a cadre of football day-trippers creates a Saturday morning stampede. Ordinary mortals with mundane errands venture out at their peril until all the visitors park their vehicles and hoof it toward the stadium.

When the game starts, an eerie calm settles over the town. Hardly a soul walks the sidewalks and only a scant few cars travel the roads. Footsteps echo in the big box stores. But if the wind is in the right direction, the roar of the cheering crowd wafts its way through the crisp autumn air to my neighborhood a mile away.

In about three hours, the competing teams manage to sandwich sixty minutes of play in among time-outs and a half-time show. The game is over. The hyped-up crowd vents its energy. Winners carry their coach high above their heads around the field. Compatriots charge forth to attack the goal posts. The fact that I haven't heard of any downed goal posts in the last few years attests to the ingenuity of campus police and maintenance crews. As merriment rivaling a Roman circus draws to a close in the stadium, some of the winners celebrate and some of the losers commiserate with “wobbly pop” at the local watering holes.

Some of the less rowdy and more sober spectators begin a mass exodus out of town. Traffic again traps us locals in our homes, or at least confines us to our neighborhoods. Fans who stay a second night enjoy another round of parties and create another exodus on Sunday. Regardless of when they leave, the football fans claim they had a good time and can hardly wait for the next game.

I guess I still don’t understand football.

On Living Sustainably

Biologist Garrett Hardin's parable, "The Tragedy of the Commons," captures the essence of sustainable living and demonstrates the environmental consequences of over-consumption. According to the parable, all was well in a village that maintained a common area where every family grazed one cow. Then one family got a second cow. Not to be outdone, other families followed suit. The cows overgrazed the land, the grass died, and eventually, all the cows starved. Today we affluent humans court tragedy as we demand more and more of the world's resources and cast off larger and larger quantities of garbage.

Americans make up only about 5 percent of the world population but we receive a third of the income and use more than a fourth of material and energy resources. Our culture teaches us to want things, to equate comfort and happiness with having the latest model car, the most stylish clothing, and a luxurious home. We don't think about whether we really need all these things or even whether having them makes us happier or more satisfied with life. We tend to ignore the downside–the cost in time, money, maintenance, insurance, security devices, and worry–of accumulating too much stuff.

Because we want so many material things, it takes about twenty-nine acres of usable land (An acre is about the size of a football field.) to meet the demands of one moderately affluent American–for food, clothing, housing, transportation, including that person's share of space occupied by public buildings, businesses, industry, highways, and parks. That's more than seven times the four acres per person our planet can provide.

Worse yet, most of us throw away at least a ton of trash a year, more than twice as much as the average European discards. In fact, Americans throw away more stuff annually than most of the world's people own. We not only waste stuff, we waste energy, about $300 billion worth per year, or about $3500 per person, according to *WorldWatch* statistics.

The very act of creating trash means we have disrupted natural recycling processes. Nature's recycling never generates trash. Every living organism survives on substances produced by other organisms. Animals eat plants and smaller animals. Microorganisms and small animals such as insects and worms digest the remains of dead plants and animals and produce carbon dioxide and water. Plants complete the cycle by using these materials in the presence of sunlight to grow or make new plants.

Unless we learn to limit our demands for goods and energy, one of two things will happen. Either our ecosystems will collapse and leave us struggling for mere survival or we will learn to live sustainably. Living sustainably will be much less painful. We can start by being more selective about what we buy, more wary of sales pitches that make us want things we never knew we needed. We can limit how much imported food we consume by paying attention to where foods come from when we make a vicarious round-the-world trip through a local grocery store–European cheeses, Asian tea, African coffee, South American grapes, Costa Rican bananas, Alaskan seafood, and produce from the irrigated valleys of California. According to *WorldWatch*, refrigerating, transporting, and storing food can use as much as eight times the energy provided by the food itself. We can eliminate much of that by selecting locally grown foods wherever possible.

We might also move toward a "waste not, want not" life style that most farm families followed when I was growing up on an Indiana farm in the 1930s and 1940s. We got most of our food right from our own farms–eggs, milk, fryers, an occasional pig or steer, and a large vegetable garden. We generated very little trash and we lived quite comfortably because we didn't miss things we never had.

In recent years we affluent Americans have made significant progress in recycling newspapers, office paper, magazines, empty glass and metal containers, some plastic containers, plastic bags, aluminum foil, and corrugated cardboard. These efforts shrink our garbage pile but they fall short of the efficacy of nature's own recycling program.

The purpose of this essay is to show how we as individual citizens can move toward sustainable living. Business and industry must also move toward sustainability, but right now I want to focus on what we as individuals can do. Much of the information I will present comes from the *Consumer's Guide to Effective Environmental Choices* presented by the Union of Concerned Scientists. The *Guide* points out that we can make significant progress toward sustainability by changing how we use cars and light trucks, how we get our food, and how we manage our household operations.

###

The first way to move toward sustainable living is to limit how much we use vehicles powered by fossil fuel. On average, a car or light truck running on fossil fuel produces about two metric tons of carbon emission per year–more for SUVs and less for compact cars. Most of that carbon is emitted in the form of carbon dioxide, the most ubiquitous greenhouse gas, and thus, the most responsible for global warming. (See the essay "The Icarus Syndrome" for a discussion of the consequences of global warming.)

Engines that run on fossil fuels also emit pollutants such as nitrogen oxides, sulfur dioxide, ozone, and fine particulate matter into the air we breathe. Nitrogen oxides and sulfur dioxide contribute to acid rain, which damages plants, especially coniferous trees, and alters the acidity of lakes and streams. In fact, acid rain has rendered some lakes so acidic that virtually nothing can live in them. Particulate matter and ozone have even worse consequences when inhaled by humans. The *Guide* says that "in California alone as many as three thousand deaths per year are caused by particulate matter. An additional 60,000 to 200,000 cases of respiratory infections in children and up to 2 million nonfatal asthma attacks are due to both particulates and ozone."

Given these findings it seems that the single most important environmental action a consumer can take is to limit his or her personal use of fossil fuels, which in turn reduces air pollution and greenhouse gas emissions. Here's what we can do:

1. Walk, bicycle, and use public transportation instead of owning a car.
2. If you must own a car, choose the most fuel-efficient, least polluting car you can find.
3. If you're employed, live a close as you can to where you work and shop.
4. If you're retired, live as close as you can to places you normally visit–family, medical services, and opportunities for senior and volunteer activities.
5. Avoid recreational equipment that operates on fossil fuels.

###

A second way to move toward sustainable living is to reverse the trend toward factory farms and "big agribusiness."

A factory farm raises a single kind of animal and treats those animals as meat-making machines. The animals are crowded together in small pens where they often wade in their own excrement and receive antibiotics to prevent the spread of disease. Regular use of antibiotics increases the resistance of microorganisms to the drugs and over time makes them less effective in both animals and humans. Instead of using animal wastes to fertilize fields, factory farms dump wastes in excrement ponds. The ponds emit an almost unbearable stench and they often leak wastes into local streams. Such wastes can easily pollute drinking water for towns and cities downstream.

Eating meat has several disadvantages. Red meat contributes to the risk of heart and blood vessel disease. All kinds of meat, poultry, and fish can increase the risk of taking in toxic chemicals and infectious agents. Treating plants with pesticides means that animals that eat the plants concentrate the chemicals in their tissues. Pesticides become further concentrated when humans eat the animals. The increasing frequency with which meats are being recalled because of contamination in packing plants poses a risk of acquiring a disease from meat that slipped through inspections. Finally, because animals must eat ten to twenty pounds of grain to make a pound of meat, our planet can feed many more people if the people eat grain directly. One sensible choice, given all these potential risks, is to become a vegetarian. Worldwide, millions of people stay healthy on a vegetarian diet, especially if they include dairy products and eggs in their diet.

Even a vegetarian diet can have its problems. Over recent decades growing crops has become increasingly dependent on "big agribusiness," where a single strain of a single crop is planted in hundred-acre fields. Such fields use massive pieces of equipment, large quantities of fossil fuel, synthetic fertilizer, and toxic chemicals such as pesticides and herbicides. They often use inefficient methods of irrigation that remove water from aquifers (natural underground water stores) faster than the aquifers can replenish themselves.

Planting only one strain of a crop risks the extinction of other strains and reduces biological diversity. Such diversity would be extremely valuable if an insect pest or climate change destroyed the strain being planted. That's exactly what happened in the Irish potato famine of the mid-19th century, in which a fungus spread across Ireland destroying potato crops as it went. Many people starved or became debilitated and susceptible to diseases such as cholera and typhus. Some survived long enough to sail for America, but died when their rickety ships capsized. All told, about a million people died as a result of the potato famine and the lack of biodiversity among potato plants that allowed the fungus to attack all plants.

Today, biodiversity in potatoes is maintained in the Peruvian Andes where over 2000 genetically distinct varieties of potatoes grow. Among these varieties, some can adapt to almost any particular set of environmental conditions–wet, dry, hot, cold, whatever. Preserving biodiversity for all food crops will serve us well if monocultures or unusual environmental conditions destroy the strain of a crop being cultivated.

Genetically engineered (GE) crops are created when a genetic factor for a characteristic never before present is introduced into an organism. Maintaining natural genetic variability is essential for sustainable agriculture, but geneticists working for "big agriculture" have not always used good judgment in the way they use genetic engineering. When they inserted genes that render a crop resistant to herbicides, some thought that was a good idea. The crop resisted the herbicide, but the genetic factor soon showed up in weeds, too. The weeds acquired the same characteristic and the battle between crop and weeds resumed. Next they introduced a terminator gene, one that prevents the seeds produced by a crop from sprouting. The developers thought that would increase the amount of seed they could sell, but it creates an undue burden on farmers in poor countries who depend on saving seeds from one year to plant the next year's crops.

Probably the most detrimental effect of GE crops has occurred with corn. GE corn pollen disperses rapidly to nearby natural strains, and nearly all corn strains typically used for crops already contain GE genes. When GE corn intended for food was inadvertently planted in Mexico, the resulting plants dispersed pollen with GE genes. This pollen threatened the genetic uniqueness of ancestral varieties of corn, which have existed for centuries in Mexico. Mexican scientists are now trying to protect ancestral corn strains from being fertilized with GE pollen. As with potatoes strains, protecting ancestral corn strains is essential to preserve diversity.

Worse than all the above disadvantages of "big agribusiness" is its need for subsidies. A study reported in *WorldWatch 2002* estimated that in the United Kingdom alone, the cost of removing pesticides and other agrochemicals from drinking water, repairing damage from soil erosion, and the medical costs of food poisoning and mad cow disease would have cost about $2 billion per year, had these remediations been attempted. The longer these onslaughts on the environment continue, the less likely it is that they can be remediated. Agribusiness seems successful only to those prepared to ignore the environmental damage it does and the cost to taxpayers to subsidize these losses.

Today, the increasing demand for organically grown crops is a welcome change because it is making sustainable farming economically feasible again. Buying organically grown produce is good for the environment because the techniques used to grow it are better for the land and far more environmentally friendly than the habitual use of synthetic chemicals–manufactured fertilizers, pesticides, and herbicides. Organic farming is environmentally sustainable. Instead of using synthetic chemicals, it depends on animal wastes for fertilizer, crop rotation, and natural pest management to limit crop damage from insect pests. It also encourages the renewal of family farming and makes healthier foods available. On family farms that raise livestock, animals graze in pastures and are not regularly subjected to antibiotics and supplemental growth-stimulating hormones.

Organic farming is the kind of farming my family and many other families practiced before synthetic chemicals and massive machinery became available. We can restore that kind of farming if we all take the following actions:

1. Purchase only organically grown fresh produce.
2. Eat vegetarian or buy only meats from free range grown animals that are free of synthetic hormones and other chemicals.
3. Support farmland trusts and similar mechanisms to keep small farms in the hands of farm families.

As essayist Wendell Berry explains in *The Gift of Good Land*, farming should be done by people who are ecologically and culturally responsible for their farms, that is, by people who love the land.

###

A third way to move closer to sustainable living concerns household operations, such as space and water heating, air conditioning, and appliances. If you are looking for an apartment, try to select one with modern, efficient space and water heating equipment fueled by natural gas or an electric heat pump. If you own your home, you can replace old inefficient equipment with new, high efficiency equipment and save the cost in a few years because of reduced operating expenses. Every year, the cost of solar and wind energy systems become a little more competitive. Improvements such as insulation, weather-stripping, and storm windows keep homes more comfortable, save on heating bills, and help to protect the environment from greenhouse gases and other air pollutants.

A word about so-called clean electric power. It is true that electric power does not pollute the area where it is used, but depending on how it is generated, it can contribute significantly to greenhouse gases and air pollution. Some modern generating stations use pollution-free solar power or wind power. According to what I learned when I visited an experimental tidal power generating station in maritime Canada, tidal power may become a future energy source. Hydroelectric power generators, which are fairly common, operate without generating pollution, but they require large dams that alter the flow of water in rivers and disrupt ecosystems. From an environmental perspective, the least desirable plants are those that use oil, coal, or nuclear energy. Oil and coal have all the drawbacks of any fossil fuel. Nuclear energy leaves radioactive wastes for which no entirely safe means of disposal has been found.

If you are planning to buy a furnace or water heater for your home, you can save money while you make your home more environmentally responsible. Here's what to do:

1. Compare the price and environmental effect of each power source in your community and select the most appropriate energy source.
2. Use the efficiency rating of various models of furnaces and water heaters to choose the most efficient one that otherwise meets your needs.
3. Regardless of whether you own or rent your home, you may need to replace appliances. When you do, select the most efficiency model that meets you needs.

Although this essay doesn't consider ways businesses and industries can become more environmentally responsible, the principles that apply to individuals also apply to them. Many enlightened managers are discovering that saving energy and minimizing waste makes businesses and industries more profitable. If we Americans and our businesses and industries became seriously committed to the principles cited here, we could move closer to sustainable living day after day, year in and year out, indefinitely. The struggle to get everybody to live sustainably creates a dilemma ably stated by E. B. White: "I arise in the morning torn between a desire to improve (or save) the world and a desire to enjoy (or savor) the world." The nearer we come to attaining a fully sustainable society, the nearer we will be to saving the world and the more we can savor it.

Life on a Human Scale

I envy the many Europeans who live in cities made more livable by providing small pedestrian centers that function on a leisurely human scale. Life in those cities is gentler, healthier, and more sustainable than in most American cities. Unfortunately, some Europeans are mindlessly "Americanizing" their cities with too many automobiles and fast food vendors. Cities with gentle ambiance still exist. You just have to look for them.

You can identify these livable cities by their pedestrian areas with clusters of large and small shops, eateries with indoor and outdoor tables, vendors of traditional foods, park benches, and lots of flower boxes, either free-standing or perched on window sills. Musicians play classical or folk music and passers-by show their appreciation by tossing coins and bills into an open instrument case. People look less harassed as they shop, and some push toddlers in strollers. Many of the shoppers seem to know each other because all around the pedestrian area I see clusters of two or three people chatting. Others rest on benches or gather at café tables. Cyclists dismount and walk their bikes respectfully through the pedestrian area. Amplified music, roller blades, and skateboards are conspicuous by their absence. These things are permitted, even encouraged, in other places, but not where they will shatter the ambience of a pedestrian area.

Another thing that makes European cities livable is that bicycles, trains, subways, buses, and trolleys provide good local transportation. It is not uncommon to see hundreds of bikes parked at the train station during a workday. Many retirees also ride bicycles. Streets have bicycle lanes. Cars, on average, are much smaller than American cars, and drivers are respectful of cyclists. In many old cities, streets are narrow–barely wide enough for a small car–but they easily accommodate cyclists and pedestrians. An entertainment facility located on the edge of one town bases its ticket prices according to the attendees' mode of transportation. Tickets prices for most events would range from $10 for people on foot, bike, or public transportation to $20 per person for those arriving in private cars. (We Americans would need a $25 category for people riding in vans and SUVs.)

Third, cities are more compact because residents live in efficient, convenient apartment buildings, usually three to five stories tall. People accept less spacious living quarters than those demanded by many affluent Americans. On the edge of town people live in row houses, duplexes, or small, detached houses on lots barely large enough to accommodate small vegetable and flower gardens. Except for the few who own country estates, Europeans don't waste much space on lawns. Instead they have fenced playgrounds for small children in residential areas and grassy, public playing fields usually within walking distance along well-maintained hiking paths. The paths themselves encourages walking, a healthy kind of exercise. As I sauntered along the narrow streets, I shuddered to think how unbearable life would be in the old cities of Europe if every bike were a car and most apartments were houses on large lots. Europe would be one big megalopolis with no farmland and a perpetual traffic jam.

We Americans could create gentle, human-scale living in our cities and towns, too. My town of State College, Pennsylvania hasn't done so, but it could. We would need to start by routing through traffic around the city. Then we would have two main one-way thoroughfares in the downtown area, one carrying local traffic in a southwesterly direction and the other carrying it in a northeasterly direction. We have two parking garages situated two blocks apart on cross streets between the two thoroughfares. We could close the two intervening blocks to traffic to create a pedestrian area bounded by parking garages at each end, the campus of our large state university on one side, and the public library on the other.

Many of the downtown shops are located in or near this proposed pedestrian area. We could ban private vehicles from this small area and still allow our city buses, which run on natural gas, to travel along the thoroughfares just as they do now. We could add a free shuttle bus that continuously circles the pedestrian area. And we could allow access to the area for delivery trucks during the early morning hours or some other limited period of time.

We already close streets in the proposed pedestrian area to traffic for special events. During the summer Arts Festival the streets are lined with food concessions. For our First Night Celebration on New Year's Eve and New Year's Day, they provide a place for ice sculptors to display their creations. People mill about enjoying the festivities during both events. This pedestrian mall could become a permanent gathering plaza complete with sidewalk cafes, ethnic food vendors, musicians without amplifiers, and lots of park benches and flower boxes. The presence of the public library adjacent to this area would invite people to browse and would challenge the library staff to create small scale, people friendly programs to complement the area.

We could facilitate bicycle travel by creating bike lanes on all the streets leading into and out of the pedestrian area and providing secure bicycle parking spaces. Of course, we would need to educate motorists to honor the lanes and treat cyclists with respect.

We could use zoning to restructure residential areas. We might limit new construction to apartment buildings or clusters of town houses, each with a public green space. We would need an aggressive program to prevent students from overcrowding the apartments and creating unacceptable noise levels. We might encourage people who now have large lawns to convert a large part of those lawns to gardens for growing fruits and vegetables. Also, we could gradually refurbish historical homes and replace other single-family dwellings with garden apartments and new "pocket parks."

I'd like to live in this kind of city. Wouldn't you?

The Message

One evening when John and I returned home from dinner at a favorite restaurant, we found a message on our answering machine. That message profoundly altered our gentle, leisurely evening.

"This is Maggie, your son Ed's neighbor. Call me as soon as you can. My number is . . ."

I grabbed a pencil, took the number down, and hastily dialed it.

"Hello," a voice said.

"Is this Maggie? I'm Ed's mother."

"Yes. So glad you called. It may not mean anything," she said, "but when I got home from work, all Ed's doors and windows were open and his stereo was blasting away. His car wasn't parked in front, and I could get no answer when I called to him from the door."

"Oh, dear," I said. At least that's what I think I said. I wasn't thinking very clearly.

"I called the police," Maggie continued. "An officer came and went into Ed's place with me. We found no signs of Ed, but nothing was missing. We just can't find Ed. The officer found your number in Ed's phone book and asked me to call you."

I thanked her and asked her to call again if she heard anything. John had been listening anxiously to the entire conversation.

"What do we do now?" he asked. We looked at each other, not knowing where to turn for help. We soon decided to call our oldest son, Ric, who lives about forty miles from Ed in a different suburb. Ric's answering machine did its thing and we told it to have Ric call us.

Next we called our youngest son, Mark, who lives in yet another suburb. His girlfriend answered.

"This is Mark's mom," I said. "We've got a problem. Ed's missing. His neighbor called to say his house is open and his stereo is on. Is Mark there?"

"Oh, dear, that's awful," she exclaimed when I gave her a chance. "Did you call Ed's work?"

"No. He's just changed jobs and we don't have the number."

"Mark probably does. I think he's in his van somewhere on the beltway. Let me see if I can get him."

That girlfriend must keep pretty close tabs on Mark because he rang back almost immediately. I explained the situation and asked, "Mark, do you know the phone number where Ed works?"

"Yes. Stay on the line. I'll patch you through to him."

Mark is a child of his time. He has all the latest electrical and electronic gadgets and it was no trouble at all for him to create a three-party connection from his van, probably done as he rolled along. He kept us on the line while he called Ed's office. All of us heard another polite answering machine and we left another polite message.

But we didn't feel polite.

"Dammit, where is he?" my husband exclaimed to anybody who was listening.

Mark said, "Let's get a list of all the information we need to file a missing person report."

I looked up Ed's social security number and together we listed his physical characteristics. About 5 feet 10 inches, 150 pounds, collar-length, light brown hair, blue eyes, and a short, well-kept beard.

"Does he still have a mustache?" I asked.

John said, "Yes."

"What's his car license number?" Mark asked, but we didn't know.

Mark said he'd go straight to Ed's place and call the police from there so he could look for more information if he needed it. His voice quivered.

"Mom, I'm worried. I'll call you as soon as I know more."

While we waited for a call, we took turns formulating plausible explanations for our middle son's mysterious disappearance.

"Maybe he just ran to the grocery and left things open," John suggested.

"Maybe he went for a walk," I said. "No, that can't be. His car would be there."

Neither of us dared say the awful things we were thinking. The thought that kept passing through my mind was that he had been mugged and robbed, and his bloody body left in an alley somewhere. We were feeling tired, but we couldn't go to bed. We couldn't have slept had we gone to bed.

"Guess we'd better stay dressed," John said.

"I agree. We may have 200 miles to drive yet tonight."

It seemed like hours but it was more like twenty minutes until the phone we thought must have died came to life with a nerve-shattering ring.

"That'll be Mark," John said.

"Hello," John and I said into different phones.

"Hello," said Ed.

"Ed!" we exclaimed at the same time. "Oh, thank God you're okay. You are okay, aren't you?"

"Yes, yes, I'm fine. I'm still at work." He went on to explain that he'd gotten a message off the answering machine at work. Checking messages is part of his job.

"Did you know your house is wide open and your stereo is playing?"

"Yes," Ed answered calmly. "I know. I left it that way. My little brother seems to have gotten in a panic over nothing."

"We're the ones in a panic," John said. "Ever since your neighbor Maggie called us."

"Mark's worried about you, too. And he's done a lot to help us find you," I said. Now please tell us why you left your house open."

"I'm airing the place out. I quit smoking three days ago."

"Great. We're glad to hear that, but why leave the stereo on?" We couldn't help asking.

"Oh, that was to make people think I was at home. I thought about telling Maggie as I left this morning. But I was in a hurry to get to work. And I thought she'd think I was kinda crazy."

Ed agreed to call Mark and Maggie.

"What a relief," John said.

"Yes, isn't it just? I guess we can finally get into comfortable clothes."

"And back into retirement mode."

On the Likeness of Driveways and Life

I've become an old hand at sealing driveways, but I was a young woman when I sealed my first one. To me, that steep driveway symbolized life's ups and downs–up on the way home and down on the way out. The morning after I finished the sealing job, I got a "downer" in the form of a rollicking case of bursitis in my right shoulder from repeatedly moving that arm to spread sealer. I made myself go to work, but the shoulder was so painful that I couldn't even crank a pencil sharpener.

The second time I sealed a driveway, my problem was not bursitis but sunburn. I needed to seal that drive after the asphalt had cured at a new house but I didn't need to pick the hottest day in August to do it. My only constraint was to get it done before winter when water would seep into crevices and freeze and thaw until it created cracks in the driveway. Sealing this driveway came to symbolize life's little problems, the ones that sort of seep inside us and tear us apart.

I had more time to contemplate the likeness of driveways and life one summer not long ago as I scrubbed away bird droppings, trimmed overhanging grass and ivy, and sealed my third and most needy driveway. The day was just right–not too hot, not too cold, and no chance of rain.

As I looked back, I realized that driveways are a lot like life, or rather life is a lot like driveways. Years ago when my children were small, the demands of motherhood tore me apart just like ice in crevices tears a driveway apart. My biggest problem occurred when I was faced with several problems that demanded attention at the same time. When our mechanically inclined, four-year-old son started taking things apart that were not his, I could help him find something better to do. When our pigeon-toed, two-year-old daughter wore an orthopedic bar to turn her feet out and she sat spraddle-legged and wailed, "I'm caught," I could pick her up and comfort her. When our placid, two-month-old son started to make his hungry cry, I could sit down in the rocking chair and feed him. What tore me apart was trying to deal with all three problems at once. That was when I felt little crevices forming in my psyche and deepening with a kind of emotional disintegration much like the physical breakdown of the driveway.

The driveways in my life haven't always been freezing and thawing or bringing bad news. Sometimes they point to safe havens. By bike, car, or on foot, family members made their way up our steep driveway in time for dinner on many a cold winter night. When one son was working as a motorcycle courier in city traffic, I always breathed a sigh of relief when I heard that motorcycle roar up the drive. Accounting for family members as each one came up that driveway warmed this mother's heart.

Sometimes the driveways that looked the most innocent came to abrupt dead ends–at a garage door or back stoop just like some events in my life. I encountered one such dead end while I was teaching biology in a community college. I always enjoyed teaching and I'm a staunch supporter of community colleges for the educational opportunities and individualized attention faculty members pay to each and every member of a diverse population of students. What annoyed me was the rigidity of policies sometimes administered by bungling bureaucrats already promoted to their level of incompetence. I taught full-time for three years. Then during the next seven years, I taught half-time and spent half-time as editor of a professional journal.

Knowing that full-time faculty needed five years' service to become eligible for promotion, I assumed that by the end of my tenth year, I surely would be eligible for a promotion. That was when I discovered I'd never be eligible because only full-timers got promotions. Now that's what I call a dead end. I backed out of that dead end job just like I back out of a driveway. I had no trouble finding another position in a different college.

Although back-out driveways can offer a fresh start in a new direction, they can also symbolize life's tendency toward catastrophe. The driveway at one place I worked was a catastrophe waiting to happen. Visibility was bad because of parked cars and trees. Small things like recycling bins, dogs sorting garbage, or toddlers giving Mom the slip posed special hazards. My nemesis was an easily visible thing, a big parked truck that was closer than I judged it to be. The accident happened in the late afternoon dusk of a mid-January day. The driveway and parking area were icy. The first I knew of the truck was when my back bumper snapped the corner off nine large sheets of plate glass specially ordered for the renovation of a nearby building. My insurance agent was amazingly consoling. He said I had saved the company lots of money by hitting that glass before the recipient paid for it so the company could settle the claim at the wholesale price of the glass.

From bursitis to my backing out disaster, events of my life involving driveways flashed through my mind as I spread tarry black stuff on my last driveway. Suddenly I saw all the similarities between driveways and life. I concluded my erratic career as a driveway sealer with a smidgen of sealant left in the second of two five-gallon cans and a monumental backache. Once I finished that job, I hit the ibuprofen and retired to the sofa, eschewing tool cleaning. I threw those tools away. I wouldn't ever need them again because I wouldn't be sealing any more driveways–never, ever again. Old backs and old driveways just aren't made for each other, and after that last driveway, I'm ready to take advantage of opportunities for life in a slower lane. But if I hadn't sealed that last driveway, this essay might not exist.

On Mozart

Wolfgang Amadeus Mozart is my all-time favorite composer. The many performances and recordings of his works available today tell me I'm not alone in my liking for his work. If I had recordings of all his works, I could play one a day for nearly two years. By that time, I wouldn't find it boring to start through them all over again. Listening to Mozart is a pleasurable pastime at any age, and it's particularly delightful now that I'm retired. Mozart offers great variety, everything from simple sonatas and effervescent chamber music to dramatic symphonies and flamboyant operas. I would need no other music for the rest of my life.

Mozart is remembered by many as a musical genius. At an age when most children are learning to read, Wolfgang was already a talented pianist and prolific composer—a child prodigy. Compared to his other talents, reading wasn't important. He wrote his first symphony when he was only nine years old. Ludwig von Köchel, who numbered Mozart's 626 compositions in chronological order, identified the first symphony as K. 16. (The "K" stands for Köchel.) The fifteen lower-numbered compositions are mainly sonatas and minuets for piano.

Mozart's father, Leopold, was a violin teacher, but his greater ambition seems to have been the exploitation of his son's talents for whatever fame and fortune he could glean. From the time Wolfgang was six years old, Leopold regularly took him on tour to play for royalty in Vienna, London, and other European cities. Little Wolfgang was wearing satin suits and learning court manners at an age when boys are more likely to be playing sandlot ball. His biographers indicate that he seemed to enjoy playing for an audience.

Born January 27, 1756, Wolfgang was the last of Leopold and Anna Marie's seven children. Only the fourth child, Marie Anna (nicknamed Nannerl), and Wolfgang survived to adulthood.

He probably inherited his cheerful childlike traits from his mother, but he hadn't slightest respect for her authority. Wolfgang never attended school, but that wasn't particularly unusual in his day. His attendance would have been erratic because most of the time he was either traveling or recovering from an illness he had contracted during his travels. Some of those diseases were serious, debilitating infections such as scarlet fever and smallpox. Because medical treatment wasn't very effective in Mozart's day, recovery was slow. Leopold, who provided what formal education Wolfgang received, described his pupil as enthusiastic and apt, obedient and good-natured.

Wolfgang acquiesced to his father's domination until he was about twenty years old when he began to flaunt his musical superiority and independence. His musical judgment was sound but much less dependable in most other matters. At that age he began to spend a great deal of time with the Weber family and soon fell in love with the daughter, Aloysia. However, the conniving Mrs. Weber managed to get Mozart to marry Constanza. another of her daughters. Mozart was 26 when he married, and the couple had four boys and two girls in the eight years before he died. Only the second and fourth sons survived to adulthood. Neither made a mark in music.

Partly due to his ineptness as a business man, Wolfgang's family life was chaotic and he was in constant need of ready cash. He spent his time composing and received only composition fees for his efforts. Given the great respect people have for Mozart's music today, it seems a cruel twist of fate that he was so unappreciated and poorly rewarded in his day. Music of the caliber Mozart composed should have provided generous accolades and a handsome living. But that was not to be.

Mozart lived to see the first performance of his last opera, *The Magic* Flute, and died nine weeks later on Dec. 5, 1791 less than two months before his 36th birthday. Biographies of Mozart often provide a picture of the simple funeral cortege that delivered his body for burial in a pauper's grave.

Mozart's works span the short period between the last of Haydn's compositions and the first of Beethoven's. Many people attribute Mozart's genius to his universality. He composed in all musical forms–minuets, sonatas, other forms of chamber music, symphonies, choral works, and operas. He contributed significantly to the development of music from an early classical style to the rich, dramatic works that foreshadowed Beethoven. A particularly notable aspect of his genius was his ability to compose entire works in his head as he rode along in a carriage. When he reached his destination, he would sit down and with apparent effortlessness write out an entire score. Mozart stands head and shoulders above most other composers in the sheer volume of works completed. That so much of his work is of outstanding quality is even more impressive.

Every music lover must have some favorites among Mozart's compositions. I especially like his clarinet quintet and a clarinet concerto, probably because as a girl, I tried to learn to play that instrument. I never got beyond mediocrity with the clarinet, but I did learn enough to appreciate the special way melodies seem to flow effortlessly from a well-played clarinet. The fluid tone and long runs that cover the clarinet's nearly three-octave range never fail to send chills of delight down my spine. Mozart also wrote for other wind instruments and I particularly like his compositions that feature the French horn, bassoon, or flute.

Among Mozart's operas, I've read that musicologists would most likely select *Don Giovanni* as his best operatic work, but *The Magic Flute* is my favorite. The preposterous plot creates occasions for a variety of arias: serious duets for the lovers Tamino and Pamina, fiendishly difficult coloratura solos for the Queen of the Night, and resonating, reassuring bass solos for the high priest Sorastro. The delightful birdman, Papagano and his girlfriend, Papagana, provide charming comic relief.

More than two hundred years after his death, Mozart's chamber music, orchestral works, choral works, and operas still display the freshness of genius and continue to thrill live audiences. They also flow out over airwaves across the globe and from thousands of compact disks in homes and vehicles or from portable players hooked to the belts of joggers. Those of us who love Mozart's music experience a flutter of excitement every time we hear familiar strains of a favorite work.

On Playing the Recorder

I get great pleasure from playing a musical instrument whenever my mediocre talent allows. Recorders, being the most forgiving of instruments, allow it. One needs little talent to learn to play a recorder and not much of a musical "ear" to play in tune with others. For an amateur like me, even a modicum of success is exhilarating. Playing a recorder is a perfect addition to slow-lane living.

For my first recorder lessons, I selected a tenor recorder. I'm not quite sure why, but maybe I considered the fact that the soprano recorder makes such a shrill sound it hurts my ears. Maybe the group needed a tenor recorder for balance. Anyway, I started learning to play the tenor recorder. Although a few people have large enough hands, I found that completely covering the holes in the body of the instrument was quite a stretch. The joints in my fingers ached for the first several weeks I played. And they do it again whenever I go back to the instrument after not playing for a while.

What lessons I've had were with a group of adult students, some as green as I. We started out playing short simple tunes, in which each instrument–soprano, alto, tenor, and base–played a different set of notes. We enjoyed harmony, both musical and psychological, in our group from the beginning. We all got a thrill from playing something that sounded good. Our standards weren't very high, so we were easily pleased.

After a set of lessons we kept our group together and even played in public a few times. Then our leader moved on to more challenging activities, and our group fell apart. She had already given much of her time for us, and her talents were far superior to ours. We could all see that she had better things to do, and I suspect that she was somewhat embarrassed to be identified with such mediocre musicians. I have often thought I might try to reconvene the group, but so far my inertia has exceeded my enthusiasm and I've taken no action.

Even when I have practiced alone, I've gotten a great sense of accomplishment from a modest degree of mastery of a few pieces. Playing alone was challenging, but playing in a group was much more interesting and rewarding. Listening to ourselves and hearing how we got a little better each week was its own reward. Playing in a recorder group was a supremely satisfying thing to do.

After playing the tenor recorder in our group, I bought an alto recorder and tried learning to play it. The principles are the same regardless of which recorder one plays. With a little more effort I could have learned the basics of both instruments. One reason I wanted to be able to play two recorders was to be prepared if I encountered someone with whom to play duets. If that person could play either an alto or a tenor recorder, we would be in business. Alas, no such person has come into my life. So my recorders rest in peace on a closet shelf just waiting for the right moment to come out and make music again.

Pajamas, Good Books, and a Fire in the Fireplace

Pajamas are the perfect attire for any and all at-home time. A good book is a joy whenever and wherever I have time to read. A fire in the fireplace warms my body and my heart. The combination–wearing pajamas and curling up with a good book in front of a crackling fire–is an unbeatable pastime.

Proper pajamas are big and baggy. They never bind. I'm completely comfortable and decently covered when I wear them. Now that my husband and I are retired and don't often go out in the evening, we think of pajamas as our own special kind of evening attire.

I like to put my pajamas on as early in the evening as possible. On cold winter nights, I warm those pajamas over the bathroom heater before I put them on. Unless I need to go out early in the morning, I wear my pajamas 'til nearly noon. Compared to pajamas, street clothes seem like mandatory manacles and are to be avoided whenever possible, even at the risk of occasional embarrassment.

Embarrassing situations do happen. Sometimes people come to my door after eight in the evening or before eleven in the morning. When I open the front door, they see me in pajamas and robe. Their eyes bulge and their eyebrows rise.

"Oh, dear, I hope I didn't wake you up. I hope you not sick," they say.

"No," I assure them, "you didn't wake me up. No, I'm not sick. I just enjoying wearing pajamas any time I can."

As a connoisseur of pajamas, I have some strong views about which pajamas are acceptable for each season of the year. Summer pajamas must be sleeveless and have short pants. They must be made of light-weight but not "see-through" material, 100-percent cotton, the original fabric that really breathes. I want nothing to do with sticky synthetics when the weather is hot and humid. I like bold prints for summer, even those with gaudy red flowers and sleek golden tigers. I don't mind that look like they came from a steamy jungle as long as that's as close as I ever get to a real jungle. Pajamas for spring and fall are also cotton, but they have short sleeves and long pant legs. At some point the pants become cut-offs and take on the status of summer pajamas.

Winter pajamas, in contrast, should have long sleeves and long pant legs. Sometimes on especially cold nights I wish my pajamas had feet in them like the ones I had when I was a very little girl. Flannel is the only proper material for winter pajamas, and the fleecier the better. Most any decoration is acceptable. Prints, stripes, and plaids, they're all okay, as long as the fabric is soft and cuddly. Maybe it's a sign of my second childhood, but I could really "dig" some new pajamas in a teddy bear print on fleecy blue flannel. They would be perfect for curling up with a good book and a cozy fire. (Thanks to the fact that my daughter read a draft of this essay, by the next Christmas I had those longed-for pajamas.)

I like reading a good book. My tastes run to nonfiction more than fiction, and I like biographies and personal essays best of all. Occasionally I read a novel, and I usually read a few pages of a murder mystery the last thing before I go to sleep each night.

With a good book, I get so engrossed, so absorbed that I lose track of time and place. Many people say they do that when they are reading a novel. Yes, I, too, am mentally transported to the setting right with the characters when I read a good novel. While I was reading *The Poisonwood Bible*, I didn't much like the characters and I would have been very uncomfortable in the setting. But I couldn't put the book down. I had to know what happened next. I wasn't even particularly satisfied when I finished the book; I was just relieved that I had finished it. All the way through the book, I kept wanting to fix the characters, to make the father less pigheaded and the mother more realistic. I wanted her to take herself and her girls home before tragedy struck, but then there would have been no story to tell.

Biographies, especially autobiographies and memoirs, are also often hard for me to put down. I've recently read two autobiographies that I found every bit as gripping as any novel. Marvella Bayh's autobiography is a portrait in strength and dignity. She spent years working with her husband Birch Bayh helping him get elected to various offices including that of U. S. Senator. Now her son Evan holds the same position. Marvella fought her own courageous battle against breast cancer to the very end, all the while working to prevent other women from suffering her fate.

Jocelyn Elders's autobiography portrays another woman with no lack of courage. She gives a spellbinding account of her early years in almost inconceivable poverty, how she cleaned houses to pay her way through college. The story follows her path to and through medical school in Arkansas and her carving out a professional niche as a teacher and researcher. Throughout her career she coped with burdensome personal and family problems and she fought a double whammy all the way–being discriminated against both as a woman and as a black.

In addition to autobiographies, I like personal essays. They are short enough to enjoy in odd moments and challenging enough to be worth thinking about later. Ellen Goodman has always been one of my favorite essayists for her timeliness, brisk style, and punch-line endings. Now Molly Ivins gives her some stiff competition. Being a scientist myself, I like the essays of other scientists. Essays by Margaret Mead, Loren Eisely, and Stephen Jay Gould always include some thought-provoking ideas. And physician Lewis Thomas' essays have a grace that never fails to charm me.

I could read E. B. White by the hour. His masterpiece, "Once More to the Lake," describes a summer vacation White spent with his young son at the same place in Maine where he had camped as a boy with his father. The setting was so much the same thirty years later when he took his own son there that he often slipped into the illusion that he *was* the boy and the man was his father. White's essays have stood the test of time, and many of them are as fresh now as when they were written.

Fireside is the best place to sit and read a book. To make ready, I get into my pajamas and set out my book. Then I lay a fire with deliberation. First I open the chimney damper. Forgetting that step leads to a very smoky room. Next I build a pen of kindling around a small "starter log" and top it off with two regular logs. I grab a section of newspaper, mold into a bouquet shape, set the outer edges alight, and hold it high inside the fireplace to warm the chimney. When the flames begin to singe my knuckles, I let go. The flaming bouquet ignites the starter log. Once the fire is going, I can sit back, relax, and soak up the warmth as I read. Sometimes I get so engrossed in the fire that I put my book down and concentrate on the fire.

Fingers of bright yellow flames flicker and make whish-whish noises as they lap up over the surfaces of a log and greedily nibble it away. After a while, gray bars of ash create intricate patterns in the bark. Soon the bark turns uniformly white and crumbles away from the log. Solid wood that was once protected by bark begins to burn.

I pick up my book and read some more. When I hear a log shift position, I look up and notice that the logs are shrinking. Flames have burned their way through kindling strips that now make a bed of glowing embers on the floor of the fireplace. The surfaces of the logs heat up and blue flames creep out from under the crackling logs. The room gets warm and cozy.

With the kindling spent and the bark gone, the fire slows its pace. The moment I've been waiting for comes when I feel the supreme kind of relaxation that comes to me only when there's a fire in the fireplace. I get sleepy, doze off, and drop my book. Flames continue to flicker along the burning surfaces. The fire alternates between dull hissing sounds and sharp crackling noises that rouse me to pick up my book. Delicate puffs of steamy sap rise from the logs. When the wood gets red hot, its surfaces seem to glow and pulsate in shades of red from dark to bright. Chunks of charred wood fall away and add themselves to the rapidly growing bed of coals. I sit motionless until I'm almost mesmerized by the rhythmic flickering.

When the flames begin to tremble as they flicker, I get up and throw another log on the fire. I'm awake now. I find my place and go back to reading. Fresh yellow flames leap up to attack the newcomer. Soon it, too, is covered in ash that turns from gray to white and litters the red coals. Eventually, yellow flames subside and are replaced by smaller, more intense blue flames. Gradually, the original logs turn to red-hot pencil thin sticks, then crumble into coals.

The last log now rests on the bed of coals. The coals themselves seem to pulsate more slowly now. I use a poker to break up the thin rails and stir up the coals. Crackling and hissing begin anew but soon become gentler heat waves that last only a little while.

Now the fire is dying and I'm dozing off again. A few puffs of steam. A crackle or two. Then nothing. The once red coals turn white with ash and crumble. Slowly, the life of the fire ebbs away. I put away my book, close the fireplace doors, and go to bed.

Coping with Terrorism

My husband and I were on our way to the airport intending to enjoy traveling through Europe when the first terrorist plane hit the World Trade Center. At first I couldn't believe that such a devastating act of terrorism had occurred. It wasn't the sort of thing I expected to mar the peace in the richest country in the world. Nor did I expect it to mar the tranquility of my retirement years. But my own pleasure was irrelevant compared to the stark tragedy that killed so many and forever changed the lives of us all.

A week later, with new reservations and some old-fashioned trepidation, we set out on our trip. We visited capital cities such as Stockholm, Helsinki, Oslo, Copenhagen, Amsterdam, Berlin and charming, smaller towns, such as Odense, Denmark and Gimmelwald, Switzerland. Almost everywhere we went we were touched by the flowers and messages of sympathy displayed in front of American embassies or in front of the local town hall. I was disappointed to read in the *International Herald Tribune* that many Europeans thought that if America's leaders hadn't antagonized so much of the world with their autocratic behavior, our country might not have become a terrorist target. And I was saddened and ashamed to realize how unattractive America's image is abroad.

We were still in Europe when the bombing began. I can understand that one response to the terrorist acts might be retaliation, but the way the Bush administration went about it made me feel that our leaders were doing everything they could to further tarnish our image. They seemed not to be thinking very clearly about the possible consequences of their actions. It seem to me that the Afghan people were victims of both bin Laden and U. S. military action.

Back home in Pennsylvania, I was surprised and puzzled to see so many flags on display. Some people seem to think that we were obligated to support our leaders no matter what they did and that displaying flags was the patriotic thing to do. I thought citizens in a democracy should speak out against threats to that democracy. If I could have been sure that displaying the flag meant that citizens trusted their leaders to seek peaceful solutions to the problems of terrorism, I would have participated.

I was every bit as horrified, saddened, and angered as any other person by the terrorists' brutal acts. But my own country's actions seem to be designed to escalate conflict rather than to move toward resolving it. I expected our leaders to identify and remove terrorists with more precision and less damage to innocent people and property.

I am still bewildered by the Bush administration's response to terrorism and how its sudden shift of attention from bin Laden to Saddam Hussein fits into the plan. I have yet to hear a convincing justification for attacking Iraq. Many countries seem to have weapons of mass destruction and also harbor terrorists and they certainly threaten world peace. Nonetheless, I keep hoping these problems can be resolved by following the lead of the United Nations. If we in the United States want to improve our image in the world, we could show ourselves willing to exhaust all avenues of negotiation before resorting to military action.

If our effort to remove Hussein has anything to do with gaining access to oil, we could avoid war and use simpler, more peaceful ways to free ourselves from dependence on foreign oil. First, we could sign on to the Kyoto Accord to alleviate global warming. Second, we could focus on developing solar energy, wind energy, and other clean, efficient energy sources. In addition to reducing our dependence on foreign oil, these technologies also offer the promise of reducing the environmental threat of global warming. Furthermore, profits from expanded generation of solar and wind energy could improve our economy. For every gallon reduction in the amount of gasoline we use, we reduce the amount of greenhouse gases our country releases by at least five pounds.

According to the proclamation of a group of Nobel prizewinners in December, 2001, only three months after the attack, the greatest danger to world peace is the demands of the poor and disenfranchised–the 2.8 billion people (45 percent of the world's population) who live on less than $2 per day. People suffering such deprivation tend to give up hope for a better life and strike out wherever they can. The Nobel laureates recommended that to prevent mass riots, affluent countries must take cooperative, international, and democratic actions to improve conditions for the world's most needy people.

We Americans could do this by increasing our foreign aid to poor countries. Perhaps President Bush thought he was helping when he signed a bill authorizing the fast track development of international trade agreements. Although that bill gave American corporations freedom in how they trade with developing countries, it failed to protect the markets of poor countries and the rights of the world's neediest citizens against exploitation by powerful corporations..

The United Nations Human Development Report of 2002 showed that U. S. foreign assistance came to $9.9 billion for the year. That amount was second to Japan's $13.5 billion in total dollars. But as a percent of gross national product (GNP), the U. S. gave only 0.1 percent to help the world's poorest people. That's one-tenth of a penny on the dollar. It amounts to only half of what our country gave ten years ago and is the smallest percentage donation of any industrialized nation. The highest donations in percent of GNP came from Denmark (1.06), Norway (0.91), Netherlands 0.79), and Sweden (0.70). These are the only four industrialized countries that met the United Nations target of at least 0.7 percent of GNP.

Some conservative members of the U. S. Congress opposed donations because they feared they would go to enrich corrupt leaders. However, it is possible to make sure the donations go toward projects that make a positive difference in the lives of the poor. The Brookings Review (Summer, 2002) reported that donations are most effective when they provide humanitarian relief, family planning, and reductions in infant mortality. Such donations are least effective when directed toward improving the economies of poor countries.

In allocating foreign aid, the United States must consider the plight of so-called young rogue males ages 15 to 30. In many countries of the Middle East, Africa, and Southeast Asia, these males number more than 70 percent of their country's over-30 male population. Most of these young men are unable to get an education, a good job, or establish families. Because they have no hope of a better life, they are easily recruited by leaders who advocate terrorism. We ignore the plight of these males at our peril.

The Peace Corps is an especially effective organization for improving conditions for disadvantage citizens of poor countries. Since its inception in 1961, over 168,000 Americans have served in 136 countries. Data from the fall of 2002 showed that 6,678 volunteers were serving in 70 countries with a budget of $275 million for the fiscal year. That means a volunteer gives of his or her talents for a year at a cost to taxpayers of slightly more than $4000.

Most Peace Corps volunteers are recent college graduates, but six percent are over 50 and the oldest volunteer in 2002 is 83. Volunteers receive training and assignments based on their interests and abilities in such diverse areas as education, business, environment, agriculture, health, and community development.

It seems to me that one of the best ways we Americans can improve our image around the world is to increase participation and visibility of Peace Corps volunteers. Many of us senior citizens could help make it happen and enrich ourselves in the process. We could double the Peace Corps effect with a budget of about half a billion dollars. Compared to the cost of war, that's a real bargain.

Domestic programs to benefit poor Americans are suffering budget cuts now that Republicans control the White House, the Senate, the House of Representatives, and apparently the Supreme Court, too. According to the Congressional Budget Office, funding for national defense stands at $392.7 billion for fiscal 2003, an increase of 13 percent over fiscal 2002 and homeland security increased to $23.3 billion, a whopping 32.8 percent. Funding for domestic programs dropped from $362.2 billion to $354.4 billion in the same time period. Given that funding for the National Institutes of Health and special education increased, other domestic programs have been more aggressively cut.

Programs like Temporary Assistance to Needy Families (TANF) and Women, Infants, and Children (WIC), which provides supplemental food and nutrition education for children and pregnant women, are likely to suffer the most severe cuts. These programs are especially important because they serve people who have the least power to change what happens to them. Even if President Bush's goal of leaving no child behind educationally receives adequate funding, many children may very well be left behind in terms of having a safe place to live and enough nutritional food to stay healthy. Only time will tell how well poor people fare in the United States at a time when wealthy people are receiving generous and unprecendented tax cuts.

It seems to me that we still haven't learned the lesson the terrorists were trying to teach us. By attacking the World Trade Center and the Pentagon, the terrorists focused their wrath on wealthy corporations and on our military establishment. Suicide bombers may be beyond rational thinking, but thinking people should be able to see that along with tragedy, the terrorists sent us a message: Stop allowing a few people with power and wealth to deprive much of the rest of the world of the basic necessities of life.

Righting Wrongs in a Democracy

There was a time when the U. S. Constitution protected the rights of citizens from the abusive use of power and other wrongs of its leaders. It worked as our country's founders intended until recently, but it's not working now for two reasons. First, our government leaders have allowed terrorists to scare them into passing legislation that deprives citizens of their rights. Second, we, the citizens, have allowed our freedoms to be abridged by failing to maintain vigilance over our leaders and especially by failing to vote every time we have an opportunity. Our leaders used the threat of terrorism to push both the PATRIOT Act and the Homeland Security Act through Congress. In passing those bills, the Senate and the House of Representatives forfeited freedoms guaranteed by our Constitution.

The PATRIOT Act gave the government power to spy on private citizens without needing to show probable cause, simply by claiming the desired information is needed to cope with terrorism. It allows the government access to information about every citizen–financial and medical records, e-mails, student records, even what books we've checked out of the public library–without needing to show evidence that a citizen poses a terrorist risk. It also allows searches of citizen's homes without warrants and jailing of citizens without specifying charges. To get some idea of what we've lost, compare the above items with the guarantees in our Bill of Rights.

The Homeland Security Act also allows corporations seeking government contracts to receive services provided at tax-payers' expense even though the corporations maintain offices outside the United States for the purpose of avoiding federal taxes. Employees of Homeland Security can be denied many of the rights guaranteed to civil service employees. For example, employees transferred to Homeland Security can be prevented from joining a union, dismissed, transferred, or demoted without due cause. No whistle-blowers are allowed.

Much of this legislation was passed so quickly that ordinary citizens didn't have time to follow what Congress was doing, much less protest it. Even members of Congress were pressed into voting on these bills without adequate time to read and consider them.

That's not all. Our government can now declare anyone, even an American citizen, to be an enemy combatant. That person can be jailed indefinitely without being charged with a crime and without being able to contact a lawyer or come before a judge. Even though the CIA has not been able to locate bin Laden, it can now assassinate, or as Leonard Pitts says, "disappear" anyone suspected of being an al-Quaida operative. Our government now has the power to take all these actions against citizens without showing cause.

Even before the September 11 disaster, the Bush administration had ignored the Constitutional provision for separation of church and state. It violated the Constitution when it offered tuition vouchers for church-related schools and government funding for faith-based charities. It did it again when it allowed posting of particular religious documents and symbols on government property.

Some of the most disturbing events in today's terrorist-controlled public arena are that anti-abortion forces use terrorist tactics to threaten pro-choice citizens and President Bush diverts funds already committed by Congress for international family planning. These actions fail to uphold the rights of women, both in America and in poor, overpopulated countries. Furthermore, it doesn't prevent abortions as proponents claim. It actually increases the number of abortions performed because many women must chose between continuing a pregnancy or getting an unsanitary abortion so they can afford to feed the children they already have. Worse yet, it makes life even more hopeless for the very poor and drives them closer to joining the terrorists.

Why aren't more Americans speaking out against these violations of our rights? It looks like too many of us have been cowed into accepting violations of our rights in exchange for actions we've been told will protect us against terrorism. Too many of us accepted the notion that to be patriotic, we had to accept whatever our leaders told us. That's no way to manage a democracy. We must constantly monitor the actions of our leaders and protest any infringements on our rights.

We Americans have become lazy about maintaining our democracy. To change that, we must make two admissions: First, we must admit that although our country has the most wealth of any country it is no longer a world leader in some important areas. We're far behind most European countries, Canada, and Japan in providing adequate housing, health care, and education for all our citizens.

Second, we must admit that we now live in a plutocratic oligarchy, not a democracy. A hundred million Americans didn't vote in the 2000 election. It seems they thought their vote wouldn't make any difference. Such irresponsible behavior among citizens of a democracy makes it easy for wealthy corporations and individuals to usurp control of the political process. The less attention citizens give to political campaigns, the easier it is for big dollar donors to have too much say about which candidates get elected and what issues they will support when they do. So voting does matter. If we want to live in a democracy we must register to vote, pay attention to the issues, and on election day, get out and vote.

Legislation labeled campaign finance reform went into effect after the 2002 election, but I fear it left too many loopholes to be really effective. What we really need is publicly funded campaigns across the United States like those operating in Maine, Arizona, Vermont, and Massachusetts. In these states prospective candidates must qualify for public funding by collecting signatures and small one-time contributions, typically $5, from voters whom they will represent if elected. Candidates must also agree to limit their campaign expenses to whatever public funding they receive and *not* to accept additional donations. Candidates who refuse to accept these limitations are free to raise as much money as they can, and their publicly funded opponents will receive additional funding to help them compete with the privately funded candidates. Voters will know which candidates are accepting private money.

In Maine and Arizona, where public funding has been in effect for a several years, many more people, including women and members of minorities, have run for public office. Most candidates agree that public financing frees them from fund raising and allows them to spend their time talking about issues with the people they will represent.

Public funding encourages voters to take an interest in campaigns because the candidates will be working to pass legislation that benefits their constituents and not the private interests of wealthy donors. It allows citizens to take back the electoral process and make elected officials answerable to the voters. Once our country's destiny is again determined by the voters and not by powerful, private interests, our elected representatives will be able to work toward an environmentally and socially sustainable economy–one concerned with living wages, access to health care and education, and other factors that matter to voters. Publicly financed campaigns will go a long way toward righting the wrongs of our democracy.

However, our democracy won't really be safe until some serious international problems are addressed. We must work with the United Nations to foster international cooperation. For example, as the Chinese become more affluent and buy more meat and cars, their demands on the world economy may escalate prices and prevent the world's poorest people from obtaining enough food to ward off starvation. Because ten percent of landowners control forty percent of the world's tillable land, such people won't be able to acquire even a small plot of land on which to grow food. In many countries education seems to be reserved for the affluent, and especially for males. Many African girls cannot go to school, and half the women in India are illiterate.

As a scientist, I'm outraged by scientific illiteracy at home and abroad. When I recently attended a hearing about a proposed highway, some of the citizens who spoke demonstrated their ignorance about maintaining habitats and preserving diversity of living things. Too many of our citizens and our leaders don't understand basic scientific concepts. The don't understand why evolution is science but creationism is not. They cling to the erroneous notions that ignorance about sexual matters prevents teen pregnancy but solid scientific information does not. They don't understand why genetically modified crops or nuclear wastes are serious problems. Worst of all, by the time people and their leaders recognize these follies, it may be too late to save the very features of our environment that guarantee our own survival.

The only thing that sustains my hope is that historically unjust political regimes eventually tumble, especially when dedicated citizens pushed hard enough as happened in Romania, Poland, and the U. S. S. R. More improvements are needed to create healthy economies and environments in these countries, but some progress is being made. Apartheid cracked in Africa and slavery was abolished in the United States, even though more needs to be done to eradicate racism. We can have government of the people, by the people, and for the people, if you and I and every other concerned citizen work together to make it happen.

Clocks—An American Fetish

We Americans cherish our timepieces. We make a fetish of clocks. In fact, we are obsessed with clocks and with time. This all came home to me after I no longer had a rigid daily schedule and happened to have my watch in the shop for repairs. I discovered that I didn't miss it much, not nearly as much as I would have while I was working and raising a family in a clock-ruled life. And that set me thinking about things horological.

Not long ago, I performed the annual "spring forward" ritual to accommodate to Daylight Savings Time. I set clocks forward on the headboard of our bed, in our telephone answering machine, and in our video recorder. I reset the clock on the stove and the one on the microwave oven. By that time I was glad we have no clocks in our toaster and coffee pot. Our trusty computers reset themselves and sent us messages to say they'd done so. My husband set the car clock and we both adjusted the hands on our wristwatches. Only then did I realize that our well-worn wristwatches are our only remaining timepieces that actually have hands. Our world has been digitalized without our consent and certainly without our blessing.

With the "spring forward" ritual completed, I thought I could trust the clocks to do their jobs until time for the "fall back" ritual. No such luck. One morning in May some unfortunate commuters had an accident and an innocent neighborhood utility pole got dragged into the fracas. Wires snapped. Sparks flew. The utility company shut off the power.

Our clocks were just sitting there doing their jobs, but they also became victims. Most of our clocks stopped dead in their tracks. Some blinked 12:00, . . . 12:00, . . .12:00. Others went dark. Only the clocks in the computers reset themselves.

Watching the blinking clocks made me wonder how often a stopped clock is right. I calculated that the chance of such a clock being right to the nearest minute is only about one in 720–one minute every twelve hours. My son, Ric, who thinks in terms of more accurate atomic clocks told me that the chance of a stopped clock being precisely right is more like about one in infinity. But he was talking about the clocks astrophysicists use and how those folks are occasionally forced to declare leap seconds and to reset their clocks accordingly. Such people also concern themselves with matters like inconstancy and decay in the Earth's orbit and Einstein's relativity.

Super clocks always make my head swim, so I was happy to learn from the same son the simple fact that time zones were created, not for ordinary folks, but for trains. Before trains came into wide use, it was good enough simply to know it was noon when the sun reached its highest point in the sky. But trains needed to maintain schedules over long distances so people could know when to expect them to arrive and depart each station. Now that time zones are accepted more or less worldwide, we have schedules for airplanes that cross time zones almost as fast as the sun does, or rather as fast as earthly time zones move relative to the sun. Far from the equator time zones get narrow enough for planes to cross them even faster.

Time zones are clearly useful, but they created one curious situation: In any given time zone, the sun rises an hour later at the west edge of the zone than at the east edge. It does the same thing when it sets. I guess that means clock time and sun time are not precisely the same.

By the time (that word again) my head quit spinning from my son's stories about time, the power company had reinstated our electrical service. I performed the clock-setting ritual again. Our clocks are all correct now. But if a predicted thunderstorm strikes this afternoon and knocks out power again, I might be tempted to go on a clock-bashing rampage.

As I think about clocks and time, I realize our lives are shot through with clock and time fetishes of one kind or another. We are preoccupied with ideas about time. Take Daylight Savings Time. Does it save any daylight? No, of course, it doesn't. Everybody knows (or should know) that the amount of daylight we get is determined by our location on the earth and the earth's angle with respect to the sun on a particular day. Tinkering with the clock doesn't change that. It just makes us think we have more daylight because it makes us get up before we miss so much of it.

How about alarm clocks? We seem to use them to synchronize our morning "going to work" ritual. The main thing they accomplish is to create traffic jams. Traffic jams in turn create the need for stop lights, which of course create the need for, well, er, –timers to control how long the light stays green each direction at an intersection. As if this morning ritual weren't enough, we repeat the whole ridiculous stampede again at the end of every workday.

Maybe if we didn't have alarm clocks, we would amble off to work at different times, thereby keeping ourselves in a more relaxed, cooperative mood. At least we would avoid having traffic jams. If we didn't have traffic jams, we wouldn't need traffic lights. If people didn't all try to go somewhere at the same time, we might even have fewer accidents that damage utility poles and cause power outages.

I don't know when time and clocks became an American fetish, but it hadn't happened when I was growing up on a farm in the 1930s. Our only clock was an ornate *objet d'art*—a Seth Thomas clock that sat on top of a free-standing kitchen cabinet. The clock was an oblong, black metal box with small, imitation marble pillars on either side of a round clock face framed by a gold-colored band. A shiny black, iron horse sat atop the clock. Seth's short hour hand plodded from one Roman numeral to the next and his long minute hand pranced ahead going completely around the clock face every hour. Our lives weren't precise or hurried enough to need a second hand, and none of us even dreamed that digital clocks would replace clocks with hands.

Most farmhouse clock hands kept their paces, day in and day out, for eight days. Sometime before the eighth day, usually on a Saturday night, someone wound the clock. At my house, my grandmother did the job. She climbed up on a chair and opened the hinged, metal-framed glass door over the clock face. She picked up the clock key from on top of the clock next to the horse, inserted it in a small hole in the face of the clock, and turned the key repeatedly until it got very hard to turn. That's all it took to keep our elegant, one-and-only timepiece working reliably until the next Saturday night.

Good ol' Seth kept accurate time in spite of electrical storms and power outages. It fact, he was already keeping time before we had any electricity to go out. He taught two generations of children how to tell time. The way Seth did it, a child could develop a realistic concept of the passage of time by watching the big hand as it moved to register minutes, and revisiting the clock periodically during the day to see whether the short hand had passed another numeral that marked another hour. With a digital clock, a child can't do that.

Seth's simplicity meant that maintaining him was a cinch. Every summer, Grandma took him down from on top of the kitchen cabinet. She washed the outside of his body and his horse with a rag wrung out of soapy water. She opened a door on Seth's back and used a chicken feather she had dipped in kerosene to clean and lubricate his innards. Seth was so much a member of our family that I almost expected him to giggle when the feather tickled. Anyway, after his annual checkup, Seth ran trouble-free for another year.

Seth was the only clock we needed. The sun and the roosters let us know when to get up. We worked hard all day. Our tired bodies told us when to go to bed. We had no late, late TV shows, no stereos, no computer games to compete with the good kind of tired that came from farm chores in the fresh air.

Now that I am retired, I get up when I wake up and go to bed when I'm tired. I can't actually claim I miss those farm chores, nor will I miss any sleep over electronic attractions. I program the videocassette recorder to tape the few shows that pique my interest. They will be available tomorrow or some other day when I get around to watching them. These days I set my own schedule if I have one. I'm free at last from the clock fetish.

At least I thought so until our clock-loving son gave us a present–a clock that picks up a radio signal from the National Institute of Standards and Technology at Fort Collins, Colorado, and resets itself every night at midnight. I suppose it adds leap seconds whenever they are declared. With my lack of schedule, I really have no pressing need for a clock that sets itself so precisely to the second every day. But to be honest, that cute little clock captures my fancy. Maybe I'm not really free from clock fetishes after all. If not, checking the time on the radio clock is a pleasant and harmless one.

A Cup of Hemlock, Please

If I'm in agony and I'm not going to get well or if I soon won't know who I am or where I am, I want to end my life as quickly and painlessly as possible. Just give me a cup of hemlock, or the modern equivalent of Socrates' final potion.

Hemlock became associated with death in the fifth century B.C. when an Athenian jury found Socrates guilty of corrupting youth and interfering with religion. They sentenced him to death and meted out a cup of poisonous extract of hemlock. Socrates drank it and died in the company of his friends. Today the Hemlock Society, named for the Socrates legend, supports and advocates the right to die for people in pain with no hope of recovery. Other similar organizations include the Compassion in Dying Federation and the Euthanasia Research and Guidance Organization in the United States and Choices in Dying and Dying with Dignity in Canada. The World Federation of Right to Die Societies has thirty-three member organizations in various countries around the world.

My fellow Pennsylvanians will be glad to know that the hemlock extract Socrates drank probably came from the shrub, *Coniium maculatum*, and not from our state tree. The shrub grows wild throughout much of the world, except where farmers have eradicated it from pastures to protect livestock. A few drops of juice from *Coniium* leaves can kill a small animal. Coniium has been used to treat neuralgia and cancer pain, so dying from an overdose of hemlock might be a merciful death.

Death by hemlock can't be any worse than my mother's death. The doctors knew she had diabetes, untreatable heart disease, and impaired liver and kidney function. Yet they ordered test after test trying to find some condition they could treat, all the while prolonging her agony and wringing the last bit of quality from her life. An ambitious surgeon diagnosed cancer and operated. He found no cancer, but he did expose her to an antibiotic-resistant microbe. She got too weak to be weaned from the respirator, became comatose, and suffered from kidney failure. Still her doctors persisted with kidney dialysis, intravenous fluids, and experimental antibiotics. She died of internal hemorrhage with the respirator still running.

I'll never know how long Mom might have lived had she not followed the doctor's orders and gone to the hospital when she developed a slight fever. Her life at home had been pleasant most of the time. She moved about her house, cooked, cared for herself, and enjoyed her family until she went to the hospital where high-tech medicine went terribly awry.

A former intensive care nurse had this to say about medicine gone awry: "Authorities arrested Kevorkian for helping his patients find relief in death but not me for tormenting patients as they declined and died. I used high-tech tools on people everyone knew couldn't be helped and who didn't want treatments. I prolonged their agony, and I knew that was what I was doing."

Treatment most often goes awry for patients who avoid thinking about death, especially their own deaths. They fail to complete legal documents to specify what kind of medical care they would want, or not want, if they should become too ill to speak for themselves. Families who don't know what a desperately ill relative would want beg doctors to do everything possible to save the relative. They can't accept the notion that their loved one is dying. Likewise, some physicians won't admit they can't cure a patient and continue to order futile treatments.

Now that I'm a senior citizen, I want to make sure that neither my husband nor I are subjected to the kind of medical mauling my mother got. I love life. I will continue to enjoy life as long as know who I am and where I am, and as long as I can communicate with others, move about, read, and be reasonably pain free. If my body and mind are too worn out to give me that kind of life, I want to die as quickly and painlessly as possible. I've made sure my family and my primary care physician know what kinds of treatments I want and don't want. I bring these issues up fairly frequently so people won't forget what they have promised to do on my behalf. I've backed this up with an advance directive and a medical power of attorney. My eldest son will use them to ensure that I receive only the care I want.

Advance directives (living wills) have been legal throughout the United States since 1994. These directives allow people specify which treatments (respirator, intravenous feeding, and the like) they would want or not want, should they become unable to speak for themselves. They can also specify an agent to act on their behalf, but that agent needs a medical power of attorney in most states. Completing these documents with the assistance of an attorney in a person's home state before illness strikes helps prevent unwanted treatments and family misunderstandings when death is near. (A living will does *not* specify how a dying person's assets are to be distributed; that requires a last will and testament.)

Aid in dying has been available at least since the Greeks coined the term euthanasia, literally, good death, to refer to deaths induced to alleviate suffering. Today, items about aid in dying make the news periodically. According to Public Agenda Online, the first modern euthanasia society was founded in London (1935). Elizabeth Kubler-Ross' book *On Death and Dying* (1969) triggered debate about treatment of the dying. The American Hospital Association prepared a model Patient's Bill of Rights (1973), which included the right to refuse treatment. The first American hospice opened in New Haven, Connecticut (1974). The Netherlands Supreme Court approved voluntary euthanasia under certain conditions (1984). The Unitarian Universalist Association passed a resolution affirming the right to die (1988). By the end of that same year Jack Kevorkian had assisted in the deaths of 120 people. Oregon became the first state to legalize physician-assisted suicide (1997).

In addition to the state of Oregon, the countries of Switzerland, the Netherlands, and Belgium now allows physicians to provide aid in dying for terminally ill patients who request it. Aid-in-dying laws generally require that the physician have a long-term relationship with the patient, that the patient must have repeatedly requested aid in dying, and that two physicians must judge the patient's condition terminal. Some also impose other requirements–that palliative care be considered or that a psychological evaluation be made to assure that the patient is of sound mind.

No one should be allowed to interfere with a terminally ill person's exercising of his or her right to die. Nonetheless sometimes physicians or family members ignore advance directives or impose their own views against aid in dying. We need more explicit laws consistently enforced to prevent such interference. We also need legislators willing to pass laws that reflect the views of a majority of their constituents. Given that sixty percent of Americans say aid in dying should be available for people who ask for it, legislators should make it legal throughout the nation. Those opposed to aid in dying must be reminded that even where aid in dying is legal, no one is required to take advantage of the law.

The unwillingness of legislators to pass aid in dying laws favored by a majority of their constituents leads to extensive use of inhumane futile treatments and the squandering of vast quantities of medical resources. In the United States, approximately 200 patients per 100,000 population, or 570,000 patients exist in a persistent vegetative state, that is, they lack any cerebral cortical function. In their 1994 book physicians Hoefler and Kamoie estimate that the cost of care is about $50,000 per person per year, or a total of $28 billion for people who don't know they are alive.

Various studies over the last decade have shown that patients whose advance directive indicated they didn't want cardiopulmonary resuscitation received it anyway and half of those requesting DNR (do not resuscitate) orders were denied such orders by the attending physician. Half of these patients died alone and in pain or hooked to a machine. Nearly one-third spent most of their family's savings on medical bills before they died. A medical system that wastes resources on futile treatments and fails to provide essential services, such as prenatal care for all pregnant women and immunizations for all children, is tragically wrong-headed.

Health care costs in the U. S. are twice as much per person as in other affluent countries. Much of the difference can be attributed to excessive charges for prescription drugs and for emergency room and intensive care services. Patients who cannot be helped by these services would be better served by gentler care in hospices and nursing homes.

Legislators' following the dictates of lobbyists for pharmaceutical companies instead of the desires of a majority of their constituents causes disproportionate increases in prescription drug costs compared to increases in other sectors of our economy. The AARP recently reported that Americans with Medicare still spend nearly twenty percent of their income for medical expenses--supplemental insurance premiums, copays, prescriptions, and dental bills. One-fifth of elderly Americans with incomes below $6,720 per person spend a third of their incomes on medical bills.

Federal funding cuts have reduced Medicare payments so that Medicare reimbursement for a person's last illness rarely exceeds $10,000, but patients, families, and supplemental insurance often pay much more. Regardless of who pays, costs go up for everyone when physicians order futile treatments. Medicare patients affiliated with health maintenance organizations are less likely to receive prolonged, costly, painful, and ultimately futile treatments than those with private insurance. Isn't it ironic that cost cutting by HMOs may, in fact, be making deaths more merciful for many elderly patients?

The option of aid in dying is an idea whose time has come. Making it legal in all states would provide opportunities to alleviate suffering among patients who want it and help curtail expensive, futile treatments. No terminally ill patient would be prevented from receiving aid in dying if it is requested, and no one would be obligated to receive such aid.

On Living to a Ripe Old Age

I've been reading about aging, but not so much that I've gotten a lot older while doing so. What I've found is that experts on aging don't always agree. T. T. Perls and colleagues, writing from a medical perspective in *Living to 100*, believe that longevity genes and low blood cholesterol are the main factors in longevity. G. E. Vaillant, writing from a behavioral perspective in *Aging Well*, claims that having a wide network of friends and loving and being loved contribute significantly to longevity.

Perls observed that people who reach eighty without developing life-threatening diseases such as cancer, diabetes, heart disease, stroke, and Alzheimer's disease are much less likely ever to develop them. According to 1995 Medicare data, medical expenses in the last two years of life for people who died in their sixties were over $22,000, but only about $8,000 for centenarians.

Resistance to serious diseases may indeed be related to the presence of longevity genes, but those of us who don't happen to have such genes must focus on longevity factors we can control. For example, we can follow a diet that promotes longevity. That means eating modest amounts of poultry and cold-water fish that contain healthy fats, fat-free or low-fat dairy products, whole grain products, five or six servings of fruits and vegetables daily, and only small amounts of red meats and sugars.

Although some experts say it's okay to enjoy a glass of wine a day, they all agree that alcohol abuse reduces both longevity and the ability to enjoy life. So does smoking. Quitting smoking is beneficial at any age because the person's cancer risk starts to drop directly and within ten to fifteen years, nearly equals the risk of people who have never smoked.

Most of us shorten our lives by taking in too many calories and too much fat and salt. My mother used to say she was digging her grave with her fork, but she couldn't discipline herself to stop overeating. The older I get, the more I understand her plight. For those who have the spartan will to restrict the number of calories they eat by twenty percent, the rewards are significant–lower blood pressure, decreased body weight, and increased high-density lipoproteins, or HDLs. HDLs transport desirable fats and keep them from being deposited in arteries.

Almost everything I read about nutrition these days beats a drum for antioxidants because they inactivate so-called free radicals. Free-radicals are charged particles that accumulate with age, damage body tissues, and contribute to the development of heart disease, stroke, Alzheimer's disease, cancer, and many age-related diseases. Some physicians recommend taking two antioxidants--800 units of vitamin E and 50 micrograms of the mineral selenium daily. Taking vitamins A and C isn't necessary for people who eat five to six servings of fruits and vegetables daily. Perls recommends drinking green tea for its antioxidant and anti-cancer properties. That's probably a good idea, but I find green tea so unpleasant that I'll settle for living as long as I can without it.

Physical and mental exercise is every bit as important as diet in increasing longevity. Today's centenarians lived active lives for many years before modern conveniences allowed them to adopt a more sedentary life style. Nonetheless, all of us should get at least half an hour of moderate exercise daily to maintain muscle strength and improve our ability to deal with stress. Exercise also can prevent or delay the onset of type-2 diabetes and heart disease. Swimming, walking, rowing, tennis, bicycling (actual or stationary), cross-country skiing, and exercising with a videotape are good kinds of activity. Climbing stairs and lifting weights increase muscle mass, improve balance, reduce the risk of falling, and accelerate metabolism. Speeding up metabolism helps an obese person lose weight.

Many seniors complain of forgetfulness. Forgetfulness can be annoying and embarrassing, but it's losing the ability to plan and carry out tasks that interferes with independent living. To keep our brains active, we need mental exercise. We can work puzzles, play games that require memory such as bridge or chess, read challenging books, learn a foreign language, play a musical instrument, or write memoirs. I really liked finding "memoirs" in that list.

Vaillant says psychological health is as important as physical health, and that living a contented, vigorous, and satisfying life seems to promote psychological health. Because Vaillant interviewed many people as they aged, he was able to identify practices that contributed to healthy aging, especially if they were initiated before age 50 and continued into old age. Those practices include not smoking or stopping early, having mature coping skills, not abusing alcohol, maintaining a healthy weight, having a stable marriage, getting regular exercise, being well-educated, taking good care of oneself, and being perseverant.

Vaillant also identified predictors of enjoyable old age: being around people and cultivating the richest possible social network, loving and being loved by a special person, having the capacity for gratitude and forgiveness, learning to play and create things, having younger friends, maintaining self-esteem even as one loses self-importance, and having subjective good health. Subjective good health means not feeling sick, even though one might have arthritis or other kinds of objective health impairments.

Perls who studied centenarians said they are a heterogeneous, unpredictable lot. But he did note that most centenarians are nonsmokers, have maintained normal body weight throughout life, and have blood pressure at or below 110/80. Arthritis is the only common chronic disease among them. In general, they are an energetic lot who have usually been healthy throughout life. They experience illness only in the last few years of their lives.

Now what made me do all this research on longevity? Well, my husband and I are eighty and seventy, respectively, and we'd like to live as long as we can still enjoy life. Part of enjoying life is finding and accepting challenges that keep life interesting. One challenge I accept is working with others to help to keep our planet habitable, that is, to try to live as sustainably as possible. Another is working with organizations that aim to stabilize human population. I'm also interested in encouraging citizen participation in preserving democracy and especially in narrowing the gap between the rich and the poor.

Those of us who are retired or soon will be retired need to make sure that we do not become a burden on wage earners. As life expectancy increases, we must expect to work more years before we retire and do a better job of planning for an adequate retirement income. I would argue for the distribution of government pensions by need instead of entitlement. By giving less to the wealthy, we might guarantee that the poor and disabled live out their days in dignity.

One way we seniors can contribute to society is by doing volunteer work. We who have a lifetime of experience can improve our own satisfaction with life by volunteering our talents for others.. We can supply the human power to address social needs, including caring for young children, working as teachers, tutors, and mentors for young people, or extending careers to become volunteers in health care. We can enrich the lives of others by teaching music, dance, painting, writing, and other arts.

S. L. Ervin, writing in *The Futurist*, predicts several important changes in the lives of retirees. He says larger numbers of retirees will (1) work again, (2) maintain independence if they have technical know-how, (3) engage in regular physical exercise, (4) drive senior friendly cars, (5) vote in relatively greater numbers than younger people, (6) seek alternatives to nursing homes, and (7) force changes in health care policies.

Whatever the future holds for us retirees, Winston Churchill captured an important property of aging when he said, "The young sow wild oats. The old grow sage."

Kitchen For Sale

I'm a kitchen klutz. Ever since I started to learn to cook and bake at age ten, I've been all thumbs in a kitchen. Over the course of nearly fifty adult years of culinary frustration, I've threatened to sell my kitchen many times. Now that I'm looking for a slower paced, more relaxed life, it shouldn't be a big surprise to any of my friends that I might fantasize about putting an ad in the paper to sell my kitchen right down to the bare walls.

I'll tell you why I really do hate to cook. In the first place, kitchen work is the most tedious of all household chores. In these days of spot removers and automatic washers, laundry is a snap. Even with hanging clothes out to dry, doing laundry is nowhere near the drudgery of cooking. With a lamb's wool duster and a powerful vacuum cleaner, the weekly or whenever-I-get-around-to-it cleaning is manageable. Even strenuous chores like cleaning a bathtub and mopping a kitchen floor rank higher on my worthiness scale for chores than cooking a meal.

Second, a meal that takes half a day to prepare is gone in minutes with nothing left to show for it except dirty dishes and a few cold leftovers. I'd rather tackle a stack of mending than to make a meal. In fact, I mend other people's clothes in exchange for ready-to-eat casseroles.

A third and very depressing thing about kitchen work is that by the time I finish cleaning up from one meal, it's almost time to prepare the next. Running a kitchen is a constant hassle. I guess that's why I often solve the meal problem by making soup. I can make a lot at one time in a six-quart pan and not need to cook again until it's all gone. In fact, that's how soup qualifies as a comfort food. It's a great comfort to me to know that I won't need to cook for a while.

Following a recipe is a particular bugaboo. I never manage to plan far enough ahead to have all the ingredients on hand before I start. Deep down I don't really care enough to spend the time and effort it would take to make sure all ingredients are on hand in advance. When I'm in the middle of making a casserole or baking a cake and I run out of eggs or shortening or nuts, I don't want to stop and go to the store. Maybe I can't stop lest the baking powder spend itself in the mixing bowl. I quickly substitute something I have on hand. I usually have a jar of applesauce in the back of the refrigerator and I've found by trial and error that it makes a fair substitute for either eggs or shortening. Once when I needed nuts, I substituted two-year-old raisins hardened by neglect on the pantry shelf. Nobody got sick. Of course, my substitutions change the flavor, texture, or other qualities of whatever I'm making. Sometimes they create downright disasters, but they let me get on with the job. The results of my makeshift cooking are safe to eat, neither poisonous nor toxic. But I can't think of a time that a substitution has turned out to be a surprise improvement.

My cooking is so bad that I tremble at the thought of the next embarrassment and I try to minimize the times I need to have people over to dinner or take some marginally acceptable dish to a pot-luck. Why can't getting together with friends be just as warm, cordial, and sociable with a bowl of soup and some store-bought crackers? Why can't I be a friend without having to go through another culinary humiliation? Too often I do something in the kitchen that sets off the smoke alarm just as guests are coming in the front door. I've served tough, soggy waffles because I didn't know they needed to be reheated in the toaster and not in the microwave. I've served a casserole that was so runny it wouldn't stay on the plate. I've made muffins that were so tasteless that I threw them to the birds and bought some on the way to wherever I had intended to take them. I got the recipe for bannock that I thought was delicious when it was served in Yellowknife, NWT. When I made it, it tasted like biscuits made with half flour and half chalk dust. Back when most Catholics ate fish on Friday, I served roast beef for a large group and didn't realize what I had done until someone asked for a piece of cheese. I didn't do any of these things on purpose. In fact, after each fiasco, I try to think of ways I could avoid repeating it. After fifty years I think there is no hope for this kitchen klutz. Now, I do hope you understand why I hate to cook and how much I really want to sell my kitchen.

If my fantasy about selling the kitchen ever came true, I really wouldn't want to eat out all the time. I would have a small kitchenette, equipped to allow me to prepare anything I will ever want to make. My super efficient kitchenette will have a small fridge, a sink, and a microwave oven built into a five-foot section of kitchen cabinets. With small appliances such as a toaster, coffeepot, can opener, and hotplate, that's all the kitchen I would need for a nutritious diet. The menu would be simple. Cereal and milk or eggs and toast, juice, and coffee for breakfast; a bowl of soup, salad, and/or a sandwich with a piece of fruit for lunch; crackers and cheese for snacks; and salad, pasta or micro-waved fish or chicken, and some vegetables for dinner. I might keep gelatin, frozen yogurt dessert, and a few cookies on hand for evening desserts. That's enough variety to keep me from getting bored with the choices my wee kitchenette could offer. Anyway, I could always add a nice glass of wine for a festive touch.

Unless someone likes to cook and clean up, there's really no need for any house to have a full-fledged kitchen. Just think of the savings among the world's affluent population if every household had a kitchenette instead of a full kitchen. Houses could be smaller by at least a hundred square feet and a whole host of large appliances and the electricity to operate them would not be needed. People could dispense with full-sized dining rooms if their meals came from an efficiency kitchen. That's another two hundred square feet a house wouldn't need. Why can't meals be all chummy and cozy when everybody has a bowl of soup on his or her lap? One last benefit of the efficiency kitchen is that if we didn't have the equipment to prepare fancy, rich foods, and could discipline ourselves not to substitute fast-food fare, we might all be healthier.

I've read that the preparation and presentation of food is a creative art. Well, maybe so, but it's not my art form. All I seem to do is to create one disaster after another. I don't think I would even be pleased if I managed to do something creative in the kitchen. What I want is *out* of the kitchen. I'll go be creative somewhere else.

On the Beauty of Soup

Beautiful soup, so rich and green, waiting in a hot tureen!
Soo-oup of the evening, Beautiful, beautiful soup.

So sang Lewis Carroll's Mock Turtle. Yes, people really do make Mock Turtle Soup, usually with oxtails (tails of cattle) or boiling beef. Recipes for this and fourteen other soups are provided in the appendix. Recipes with no source given are my concoctions–things that somehow happen when I was in the kitchen.

Almost anything edible has been served up in soup by someone, sometime, somewhere. Most soups are easy to make. They are handy one-pot meals for a kitchen klutz. When I make soup I usually start with a little chicken, turkey, fish, or seafood. Years ago when I regularly ate red meat, I made vegetable beef soup and chili. Now I make vegetarian versions of these soups. Soup is just right for a slower life style. Soup is a nearly universal food for people of any age. Babies can eat it before they have teeth and elders can still eat it after they've lost theirs. Soup can appear at the start of a meal as Cold Yogurt Soup, the main course as tried and true Chicken Soup, or at the end as Fruit Soup Dessert.

Bean soup is in a class by itself. It seems to be a staple everywhere across two continents and from high places like the U. S. Senate Restaurant Bean Soup to the German *Bauern Bohne Suppe,* or Farmer's Bean Soup.

Some other soups are characteristic of particular places. Cock-A-Leekie has been popular in royal places and humble dwellings in Scotland since the sixteenth century. In the last line of Scott's *The Fortunes of Nigel*, the king says "come my lords and lieges, let us all to dinner for the cock-a-leekie is a-cooling." Aroostook County (Maine) Potato Chowder is popular in a state famous for its potatoes. Bortsch is a typical Russian soup.

Many soups are served at particular seasons of the year–spring, summer, autumn, winter, and especially at Christmas. My Spring Soup contains freshly picked early spring asparagus and spinach. Last of Summer Soup is a catch-all soup made of dabs of various vegetables–zucchini, tomatoes, corn, green peppers, or anything else that happens to be left at the tail end of a summer garden. It's never the same twice. Corn chowder is a hearty soup, just right for the first cool days of autumn. Winter Squash Soup is a nice way to serve acorn and butternut squashes. They keep well in a cool place and give a cook a way to serve something out of the garden in the dead of winter. Christmas Clam Chowder (14) is fit holiday fare. Finally, my husband and I like Seafood Soup almost any time. Like most of my soups it's never exactly the same twice, but I've included amounts of ingredients that work for us.

No matter the place, time of day, time of year, position in a meal, or even as a snack, soup is the ever ready, always appropriate, world's greatest comfort food. Enjoy it often.

Appendix: Soups for the Scaled-down Kitchen

Mock Turtle Soup

www.soupsong.com.

1 large onion, finely chopped
2 T olive oil
2 lbs meaty oxtails or 1 lb boiling beef
1 C chopped peeled tomatoes
1 garlic clove, mashed
½ thin-skinned lemon, chopped, rind and all
¼ t thyme
1 bay leaf
2 hard boiled eggs

3 C hot water
3 C chicken broth
3 whole cloves
salt and pepper
1 T flour
1 T parsley
¼ t allspice
1 C sherry

Brown onion in oil, add the oxtails and brown slightly. Add spices and herbs, then stir in flour until it bubbles, adding more oil as needed. Slowly pour in the hot water and stock and bring to a boil. Add the remaining ingredients, except the egg and sherry. Simmer for 2 hours. Remove the oxtail, cut the meat and marrow away and add back to the soup. Discard the bones. When ready to serve, chop the eggs coarsely and stir into the soup. Ladle into bowls, stir a teaspoon of sherry into each bowl, top with parsley—and put a cruet of sherry on the table, for atmosphere if nothing else. Serves 6-8.

Cold Yogurt Soup

Louise and Art Goldschmidt, *Heritage Recipes*,
Unitarian Universalist Fellowship of Centre County, PA, 1990.

½ C raisins
2 C yogurt
½ C light cream
1 hard-boiled egg, sliced
2 t salt
½ t freshly ground white pepper
6 ice cubes
1 medium cucumber, diced
1 T chopped parsley
1 t dill seed or 1 T fresh dill

Soak raisins in cold water 5 minutes. Combine all other ingredients except parsley and dill. Drain raisins and add. Mix well, and let stand in refrigerator 2 to 3 hours. Serve garnished with parsley and dill. Serves 4-6.

Chicken Soup

1 lb boneless, skinless chicken
2 carrots, sliced
parsley, paprika to taste
2 qts water
1 small onion, sliced
1 C small, ready-made egg noodles

Simmer chicken, carrots, and onion in water until tender. Remove chicken pieces to a cutting board. Add noodles to pot and boil until tender. Dice chicken while noodles cook. Add chicken back into pot. Season with salt and pepper. Sprinkle parsley and paprika on surface and serve in individual bowls. Serves 8.

Fruit Soup Dessert

1 46 oz can of grape or berry juice
2 C fresh or canned fruits and/or berries

Add sugar and spices (cinnamon, nutmeg, allspice, ginger) to taste. Heat to serving temperature. Ladle into bowls. Serves 8.

The Famous Senate Restaurant Bean Soup

First Traveler's Choice Internet Cookbook

2 pounds of small Michigan Navy Beans
1 onion, chopped
1 ½ pounds smoked ham hocks
butter, salt, and pepper

Wash beans thoroughly and run through hot water until the beans are white. Put on the fire with four quarts of hot water. Then add smoked ham hocks, boil slowly approximately 3 hours in covered pot. Braise chopped onion in butter, and when light brown put in bean soup. Season with salt and pepper. Serves 8.

Bauern Bohne Suppe (Farmer's Bean Soup)

Recipe created from memory of a soup served in a German village in 1982

2 pounds of dried beans (whatever variety is available)
1 pound salt pork, cut into 1 inch cubes
1 onion, chopped

Wash beans and place in 4 quarts of hot water. Add salt pork and boil slowly for 3 hours. Braise chopped onion and add to soup. Season with salt and pepper. Serves 12.

Cock-A-Leekie (Scotland's national soup)
Catherine Grigor, *Heritage Recipes*

1 boiling fowl	2 T rice
2 quarts cold water	2 t salt
6 shredded leeks	good pinch of pepper
1 chopped onion	1 T chopped parsley

Draw and truss the fowl, then place in a large saucepan with the cold water, salt, and giblets. Bring slowly to a boil and skim well. Add remaining ingredients. Simmer gently until the fowl is done. Serves 8.

Aroostook County Potato Chowder
Patty Zarkower, *Heritage Recipes*

4 C chicken stock	½ C diced celery
1 ½ C diced raw potatoes	¼ C diced green pepper
2 T butter	1 medium onion, chopped

Simmer potatoes 30 minutes in stock. Saute other vegetables in butter until tender. Add to broth. Thicken with 1 C thin white sauce made of:

2 T butter	1 C milk	2 T flour

Garnish with chopped hard-cooked egg and chopped parsley. Season to taste. Serves 8.

Bortsch

1 quart beef broth
2 C cooked beets, peeled and shredded
2 C chopped raw cabbage
1 C onion, chopped
tomato juice

Simmer cabbage and onions in beef broth until tender. Add beets and heat. Add vinegar to taste and enough tomato juice to give soup the desired thickness. Serve with a dollop of sour cream or yogurt. Serves 8.

Spring Soup

Fran Goodwin, *Heritage Recipes*

1 small onion, chopped
12 stalks asparagus
½ pound spinach
1 carrot, sliced
½ gallon milk
¼ C rice
3 T oil
3 potatoes, thinly sliced
salt and pepper to taste

Saute chopped onion in oil. Simmer potatoes and carrots 15 minutes. Add rice and fresh asparagus, cut into inch slices. Simmer 25 minutes. Add finely chopped spinach and seasonings. Cook 5 minutes. Just before serving, stir in milk and heat. Serves 8.

Last of Summer Soup

2 C tomatoes, peeled and chopped
1 green pepper, chopped
1 C corn, cut off the cob
Any other garden vegetables
1 zucchini, sliced
1 onion, chopped
2 potatoes, diced
salt, pepper, basil

Place vegetables in pot, add water to cover, and simmer until done. Add water for desired consistency. Add salt, pepper, and basil to taste. Serves 6.

Corn Chowder

1 small onion, minced
1 t prepared mustard
2 C corn kernels
2 C milk
dash of Tabasco sauce
2 T butter or oil
2 T flour
2 C chicken stock
salt and pepper to taste

Saute onion in butter or oil until transparent, stir in mustard and flour. Stir in corn and chicken stock slowly. Bring to a boil; cover, and simmer for 10 minutes. Add milk, salt, pepper, and Tabasco sauce just before serving. Mix well; heat to serving temperature over low heat. Serves 6-8.

Winter Squash Soup

Joan M. Sabatino, *Heritage Recipes*

2 acorn squash
1 butternut squash
2 stalks celery
1 medium onion
3 T margarine
¼ t white pepper
2 T flour
1 large carrot
2 T cumin
1 C milk (2% or skim)

Slice squash in half, remove seeds, and bake in 350 oven until tender. While squash is baking, finely chop onion, celery, carrot, (and one hot pepper if you like spicy soup). Saute in margarine. Add flour and cook gently for 2 minutes. Add water. Remove and discard squash skin. Mash squash meat until smooth. Combine squash, spices, and vegetables. Simmer for 20 minutes. Add milk. Heat another few minutes and serve. Serves 6-8.

Christmas Clam Chowder

Freya Phillips, *Heritage Recipes*

2 C diced potatoes
1 C chopped onion
1 C chopped celery, with leaves
½ t salt
½ pint heavy whipping cream
4 C water
1 T flour
1 can evaporated milk
2 8-oz cans clams

Cook potatoes, onions, and celery in 4 cups of water in a large pan for 15 minutes. Slightly mash potatoes. Stir in flour mixed with ¼ cup of the milk. Add remaining milk and clams. Cook over lowest heat until potatoes are soft. Whip the cream and blend in. Season to taste with salt and pepper. Serves 12.

Seafood Soup

2 C macaroni
2 large carrots, sliced
2 pounds seafood (scallops, shrimp, fish, artificial crab meat)
2 boxes frozen peas
About 4 C water
1 C chopped green pepper
1 no. 2½ can crushed tomatoes
basil, oregano, salt, and pepper

Cook macaroni and carrots in a large pot of boiling water until tender. Drain. Add remaining ingredients and water to desired consistency. Simmer until seafood is done. Add spices to taste. Serves 12. Freezes well.

References

Brown, L., et. al. *State of the World 2001* (A WorldWatch Institute Report). W. W. Norton, New York, NY 2001.

Epstein, P. R. Is Global Warming Harmful to Health? *Scientific American*, August 2000.

Flavin, C, et. al. *State of the World 2002* (A WorldWatch Institute Report). W. W. Norton, New York, NY 2002.

Fodor, E. *Better, Not Bigger. New Society Publishers*, Gabriola Island, B. C., Canada. 1999.

Gardner, G. Accelerating the Shift to Sustainability, in: *State of the World, 2001*. W. W. Norton, New York, NY 2001.

Hoefler, J. M. and B. E. Kamoie. *Deathright: Culture, Medicine, Politics, and the Right to Die.* Westover Press, Boulder, 1994.

Hrdy, S. B. *Mother Nature*. Random House, New York, NY 1999.

Kolankiewicz, L. and R. Beck. Weighing Sprawl Factors in Large U. S. Cities. NumbersUSA.com. 2001.

Perls, T. T., M. H. Silver, with J. F. Lauerman. *Living to 100.* Basic Books, New York, NY 1999.

Vaillant, G. E. *Aging Well*. Little, Brown, and Co., Boston. 2002.

Printed in the United States
1324400001B/154-201

9 781589 393745